Woman of the Green Glade

O Shaw gusgedawayqua by Charles Bird King, 1826.
(Courtesy Buffalo and Erie County Historical Society,
Buffalo, New York)

. . . *she is a prodigy. As a wife, she is devoted to her husband; — as a mother, tender and affectionate; — as a friend, faithful.*

. . . *As to influence, there is no chief in the Chippeway nation who exercises it, when it is necessary for her to do so, with equal success.*

Thomas L. McKenney

Sketches of a Tour to the Lakes . . . , 1827

Woman
of the
Green Glade

The Story of an Ojibway Woman

on the

Great Lakes Frontier

by

Virginia Soetebier

The McDonald & Woodward Publishing Company

Blacksburg, Virginia
2000

The McDonald & Woodward Publishing Company
P. O. Box 10308, Blacksburg, Virginia 24062

Woman of the Green Glade
The Story of an Ojibway Woman on the Great Lakes Frontier

All rights reserved. First Printing January 2000
Printed in the United States of America by
McNaughton & Gunn, Inc., Saline, MI

08 07 06 05 04 03 02 01 00   10 9 8 7 6 5 4 3 2 1

Library of Congress Cataloging-in-Publication Data

Soetebier, Virginia M. (Virginia Marie), 1930–
  Woman of the green glade : the story of an Ojibway woman
  on the Great Lakes frontier / Virginia Soetebier
    p. cm.
  Includes bibliographical references and index.
  ISBN 0-939923-77-7 (alk. paper)
    1. Ozhaguscodaywayquay--Fiction. 2. Indians of North
  America--Great Lakes Region--Fiction. 3. Frontier and
  pioneer life--Great Lakes Region--Fiction. 4. Ojibwa
  women--Great Lakes Region--Fiction. 5. Ojibwa Indians--
  Fiction. I. Title.
  PS3569.O385 W66 2000
  813'.54--dc21
                                          99-054024

Contents

For my father,

Arthur August Mattson,

who had a deep respect for, and an abiding love of,

the Anishinabe of the North.

Preface

Upon reading Hamilton Ross's *La Pointe, Village Outpost* some thirty-five years ago, I became enchanted with the story of the Irish trader John Johnston and his Indian wife Ozhaguscodaywayquay. Shortly thereafter, I discovered *Schoolcraft, Longfellow, Hiawatha* by Chase S. and Stellanova Osborn and felt that the colorful myths of the northern Wisconsin Ojibway, their eventual influence upon the poet Henry Wadsworth Longfellow, and especially the role played by Ozhaguscodaywayquay in making these myths known to Longfellow, deserved to be better known. From these inspirations has come this story of the life of Ozhaguscodaywayquay.

So, years ago, I wrote a story based on six sentences in Ross's book. Ross's recounting of the love of a thirty-year-old European trader for a Native American teenager in 1791 and her father's caution about such a disparate union had, it seemed to me, both an ageless and a contemporary quality. As time passed, I came upon books about the Ojibway and the Europeans at Sault Sainte Marie and along the margins of Lake Superior and, through these sources, I steadily learned more about the Ojibway teenager Ozhaguscodaywayquay, the European trader John Johnston, and their time. When the facts of history collided with my imagination, I changed my text to reflect the facts. The latest book I have read about Ozhaguscodaywayquay is *The John Johnston Family of Sault Ste. Marie*, written by descendants of Ozhaguscodaywayquay and John Johnston, edited by Elizabeth Hambleton and Elizabeth Warren Stoutamire, and published in 1992. This source, too, has allowed me to change my story once again to better fit the historic record. But what Ozhaguscodaywayquay was thinking and feeling I have based on my own experiences and emotions as daughter, wife and mother, as enhanced by the sense of place I developed during my sixty years of living on the shores of Lake Superior and visiting the very sites where Ozhaguscodaywayquay lived out her life. My purpose has not been to write a history of Ozhaguscodaywayquay, but rather to write a story about the life of an exceptional Native American woman.

Words of the picturesque Ojibway language have been spelled differently by different authors. For instance, Bishop Frederic Baraga, in his dictionary of the Ojibway language published in 1878, spells the name of the Indians *Otchipwe*. Frances Densmore, in 1929, calls them *Chippewa,* while today these Indians prefer to use *Ojibwe*. In this book, I have used the most common spelling, *Ojibway.* I have used Selwyn Dewdney's spellings for the various Ojibway personal names. When Ojibway words are used in this book, they are italicized on first use and defined in the Glossary which appears on page 123.

Acknowledgments

Elizabeth Hambleton of Williamsburg, Virginia, and Elizabeth Warren Stoutamire of Tallahassee, Florida, reviewed earlier drafts of the manuscript for this book and made many helpful and constructive suggestions. Elizabeth Warren Stoutamire also provided much documentary information that greatly improved the presentation of the historical details of the story. Ms. Hambleton is a great-great-granddaughter and Mrs. Stoutamire a great-great-great-granddaughter of Ozhaguscodaywayquay, and I am deeply indebted to them both for their help with this book.

The editorial suggestions of Judy Moore and Jerry McDonald have added great clarity to my ideas and writing.

Janus Storey of the Bayliss Public Library in Sault Sainte Marie, Michigan, very kindly allowed me to photograph the Johnston family artifacts which had been housed for many years in the Judge Joseph H. Steere Room of the library.

My husband, Jack, has been an enthusiastic detective in helping me search out the Johnston family graves and the Saint Croix River battleground, as well as being my photographer.

The story of Ozhaguscodaywayquay's fast is taken entirely from Osborn and Osborn (pp. 91–92). George Johnston's words to the Ojibway chieftains during the Governor Cass incident at the Sault are taken verbatim from Johnston's "Reminiscences" (pp. 608–611). The description of the second-degree ceremony of the Midewewin Society appearing in Chapter 5 came from Basil Johnston's *Ojibway Heritage* (pp. 89–90), and the content of the rest of the chapter is outlined in Dewdney's *Sacred Scrolls of the Southern Ojibway.*

Arrangements for the use of the portrait of Ozhaguscodaywayquay opposite the title page was provided by Walter Mayer of the Buffalo and Erie County Historical Society, Buffalo, New York. The letter appearing on pages 119–120 was provided by Elizabeth Warren Stoutamire and is reproduced with the permission of the Burton Historical Collection, Detroit Public Library, Detroit, Michigan. Anita Israel, Archives Specialist with the Longfellow National Historic Site, Cambridge, Massachusetts, arranged for the use of the photograph of Henry Wadsworth Longfellow and the illustration from an early edition of *The Song of Hiawatha.* Additional information, along with many of the figures reproduced in this book, were provided by Teresa Gray of the Bayliss Public Library, Sault Sainte Marie, Michigan; Jennifer Lewis of the Bentley Historical Library, University of Michigan, Ann Arbor, Michigan; and Phyllis Weaver, Le Sault de Sainte Marie Historical Society, Inc., Sault Sainte Marie, Michigan.

I thank all of the above for their help in bringing this project to a conclusion. I, however, am solely responsible for the selection, interpretation, and presentation of the historical details in this narrative of the life of Ozhaguscodaywayquay, the Woman of the Green Glade.

Introduction

In 1790, John Johnston, having just lost his position as manager of the Belfast water works, left his family home in County Antrim, Ireland, to seek his fortune in North America. Within a year, he was being drawn into the fur trade of the western Great Lakes, an enterprise in which he continued, and for the most part prospered, for the remainder of his life. At the urging of a family friend in Montreal, Johnston traveled by canoe to the western end of Lake Superior during the summer of 1791 in search of opportunities to establish trade contacts with the Ojibway Indians. This was an area rich in fur-bearing animals, a place where there were many Native Americans but few Europeans. North of the lake, Englishmen with the Hudson's Bay Company exchanged woolen blankets, kettles, axes, guns, and beads for fur from the Indians. South of the lake, independent French traders and the British North West Company engaged in the same business. The region bordering

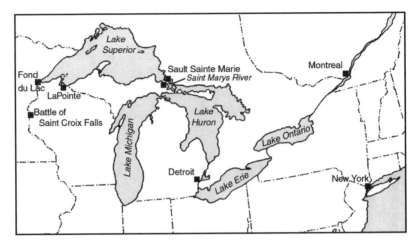

The Great Lakes of North America and principal places mentioned in this book.

the west shore of Lake Superior, however, was relatively free of established trade relations between the Indians and Europeans. Johnston hoped that he, as an independent trader, might be able to find willing trading partners among the Ojibway of Lake Superior.

Johnston spent the winter of 1791–1792 in a small cabin on what is today Madeline Island. Nearby, on Chequamegon Point, was one of the principal settlements of Ojibway Indians. In the course of interacting with these Ojibway and coming to know their leaders, Johnston became acquainted with the young Ojibway woman Ozhaguscodaywayquay, daughter of the highly respected warrior Waubojeeg. Although Johnston was very much attracted to the maiden, he also fell in love with the land itself — the dense, fragrant evergreen forests, the waterfalls crashing around and upon jagged rocks, and the endlessly changing beauty of Lake Superior, the largest freshwater lake in the world.

2

Johnston and Ozhaguscodaywayquay were married in 1792, and soon thereafter settled at Sault Sainte Marie on the south side of the Saint Marys River, a stream that now follows part of the boundary between the United States and Canada.

The Saint Marys River drains Lake Superior and discharges into Lake Huron, and Sault Sainte Marie — the name of settlements on both the north and south

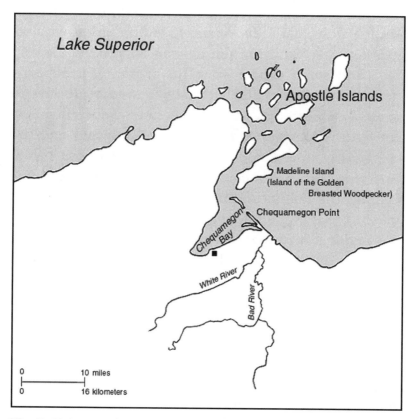

The LaPointe region was centered on Chequamegon Point and the Island of the Golden Breasted Woodpecker. The black square identifies the location of what is now the city of Ashland, Wisconsin.

3

sides of the river — occupied one of the most strategically important positions in the upper Great Lakes region. Water-based transportation moving between Lake Superior and Lake Huron had to pass near or through Sault Sainte Marie, as did land-based transportation moving between the lands lying north and south of Superior and Huron, lands that are now the province of Ontario and the state of Michigan, respectively. Clearly, the decision by John Johnston to settle at Sault Sainte Marie and open a trading post was strategically wise, and the timing was opportune.

And so, at a time when the spread of Europeans into the upper Great Lakes region was beginning to assert itself strongly, and the contact between different cultures (Native American and European) and the collision of different political ambitions (those of the emerging United States and British Canada) were unfolding, the Johnston family found itself in a pivotal role in these events at what was a major crossroads of the region. An important reason why the Johnstons did have influence was that they represented a fusion of the two cultures that were then colliding and experimenting in ways to deal with the push and pull of different traditions and the inevitable consequences that resulted from such interactions. Both John Johnston and Ozhaguscodaywayquay were intelligent pragmatists who lived lives tempered with reason and good will, and they had a realistic grasp of events that were turning about them. The strategic importance of Sault Sainte Marie benefited the Johnstons in many ways, but it also brought tension, suffering, and loss because of the political conflicts between the United States and Great Britain. The Johnstons, in turn, exerted an ameliorating influence in and around Sault Sainte Marie, often with positive consequences that extended throughout the upper Great Lakes region.

Another of the important legacies of the Johnstons's lives is that their daughter Jane married Henry Rowe Schoolcraft in 1823. Schoolcraft was an explorer, geologist, chronicler, and United States Indian Agent for the Territory of Michigan who was stationed at Sault Sainte Marie in the 1820s. His marriage to Jane brought him closer to Ozhaguscodaywayquay, her family, and the entire Ojibway culture.

Ozhaguscodaywayquay was a born storyteller. Indeed, her father, Waubojeeg, and the entire Ojibway nation were storytellers — for their history is an oral history, and the content and vigor of their experiences and traditions survived only when they were told, and retold, from generation to generation. Schoolcraft quickly came to appreciate the richness of the myths and legends he was learning from the Ojibway, the "insight they give into the . . . Indian mind — its beliefs, dogmas, and opinions — its secret modes of turning over thought — its real philosophy" (Osborn and Osborn, 409). With special assistance from Ozhaguscodaywayquay and her son George, Schoolcraft recorded his observations on Ojibway life and thought and several years later, in 1839, he published his collection in two slender volumes titled *Algic Researches: Indian Tales and Legends.*

Later, the great American poet Henry Wadsworth Longfellow discovered *Algic Researches* and other works by Schoolcraft. Longfellow then incorporated much of their content into his epic poem *The Song of Hiawatha.* He credited Schoolcraft for providing him with the information that became such an important part of this classic of American literature:

> Into this old tradition I have woven other curious Indian legends, drawn chiefly from the various and valuable writings of Mr. Schoolcraft, to whom the literary world is greatly indebted for his indefatigable zeal in rescuing from oblivion so much of the legendary lore of the Indians.
>
> The scene of [*Hiawatha*] is among the Ojibways on the southern shore of Lake Superior (Osborn and Osborn, 10).

The literary trail of Longfellow's beloved *Hiawatha* has led directly from the western end of Lake Superior, the homeland of Ozhaguscodaywayquay, into the hearts and minds of millions of school children and adult readers around the world. Ozhaguscodaywayquay played a critical role in the documentation and transfer of information about her people to her son-in-law, one of the most important chroniclers of Ojibway culture, Henry Rowe Schoolcraft.

What follows, then, is a story about the Ojibway woman Ozhaguscodaywayquay — the story about her life with John Johnston, the Irish trader; her role in helping to bridge and fuse the gap between two cultures; her management of personal, family, cultural, and political responsibilities, and tensions, amidst extended turmoil; and her legacy.

1

Dream Quest

The spring-green buds were plump on the birch and popple branches but had not yet broken out into their early lacy patterns when Ozhaguscodaywayquay, Woman of the Green Glade, left her father's winter lodge to fast. Taking nothing but her blanket, which she wrapped closely around her body, she walked a long distance while searching for just the right place on which to build her little fasting lodge. Through the forest of mixed dark evergreen and leafless trees, she came at last to the top of a long ravine where she began to pull the popple saplings down, one over the other, into the shape of a dome. Each sapling was tied to the base of another with *wattap*, roots from the pine trees that grew nearby. When the little shape was well-defined, she covered it with cedar branches woven in and out throughout the frame until she had completely covered the dome. As she worked, she thought, "I hope the grandmother will find me here. I have come a long way from Waubojeeg's lodge. But this high place must have much *manitou*. Surely I am closer to the Great Spirit here!"

As the cloudy spring day grayed to a close without a distinct sunset, she crawled into her little cedar house and curled up on yet more of the useful cedar boughs. She then covered herself with a blanket that had been bought from a trader with some of her father's finest beaver skins.

"O Great Spirit," she prayed, "Come to me here. Give me a guardian spirit, who will help me all my life. You, who give to all of us those things we need — the deer for food and skins that keep us warm, the white-fish who feed us all year long — give me now what I ask for myself alone."

And then she waited for some answer. The smell of cedar all around reminded her of her father, Waubojeeg, the White Fisher. Just a month before, he had come back from the muskrat hunt with a bad cough, which wracked him day and night. Her mother had soaked chokecherry tree bark and jackpine needles and had given him the syrup to drink, but to no avail. At last, the tribal medicine man had been summoned to administer to the chief. He had built a little cedar lodge, very much like this one of her own. A fire had been started within the lodge, and Waubojeeg had sat inside and sweated for a long time while the medicine man, accompanied by his drum, had sung the ancient songs outside the little structure. Her father had seemed a little better after this healing ceremony, but the cough remained with him still. And so the tall, slim Ojibway maiden, in her buckskin dress and moccasins, fell asleep on the first night of her fast amidst the pungent odor of cedar and the arbutus flower blossoms, letting thoughts of her father and the Kitchi Manitou mingle in her mind.

Every morning during the next few days, Ozhaguscodaywayquay would start a little fire, not only to warm herself because of the dampness and rain but also to obtain the soot she would smear on her face — for this, too, was part of the ancient ritual of the fasting time. Sometimes she would walk along the edge of the ravine, and when it was necessary, she would repair the little hut where rain had seeped through the cedar walls. But mostly she prayed — inside the hut during the seemingly incessant rain and, when the sun arrived at last, outside in the woods.

On the fifth day of Ozhaguscodaywayquay's fast, the sun shone bright and warm all the day. She sat before the hut, which was surrounded by chokecherry bushes now fragrant with blossoms; the forest seemed crowded and full, as it whitened with a million flowers. When she heard her name called, she thought at first it was the Kitchi Manitou at long last, but as the sound grew louder, she recognized it as her grandmother's voice. Grandmother was bringing water in a wooden bowl for her.

"How goes it with you, Ozhaguscodaywayquay? Are you ready to return to your father's lodge with me?" the gnarled old woman asked.

"Grandmother, I am still strong. And the Great Spirit has not yet spoken to me. Perhaps it is only that I do not recognize his voice. But still I wish to stay here longer. Perhaps he will speak louder."

"There is no shame in returning, girl, after this

9

A young Indian woman in contemplation deep in the forest (from Drake, 1848).

many days," reminded the older one as she surveyed the sooty maiden for signs of exhaustion and mental fatigue.

"No, I shall stay," said Waubojeeg's daughter firmly.

"So be it," sighed the wiser one. "But if you do not return in three more days, I shall come and carry you back with me, if I must!"

"You are so good, grandmother! You came so far with water for me. Never has it tasted so good. I will return in three days as you request. See, I will make a mark on this stick every day at sunset."

The old woman disappeared through the bushes. Ozhaguscodaywayquay continued to sit against the side of her little house, lolling in the sunshine, when a nearby evergreen tree caught her eye. It must have been of a great age for it was twisted and broken, some branches blackened as though by fire and one branch bleached as white as winter snow by a thousand suns. But decimated as the tree was, the end of a single branch that thrust outward to one side was covered by a thick tuft of green needles.

"That is the grandmother," she thought. "Her hair is white with years, her skin is wrinkled, and her hands are as twisted as the roots of that pine. Her head looks just like a turtle's, with her eyelids almost closed, and yet there is so much life yet within her, just like that one green branch there! Is it not the grandmother who brings me water and who cares now for her grandchildren, even as that one branch nourishes the tree and will put forth a cone filled with seeds to populate the

11

earth here? And did she, too, not fast as I am doing, when she became a woman?"

And at that moment, Ozhaguscodaywayquay became one with women everywhere as she recognized her role in the drama of life — a role which went on, always fruitful, despite hardships, in the lodge of Waubojeeg and indeed as it did here on the forest floor and in the deeps of the great lake, Kitchi Gami. In the spring warmth she began to fall asleep and, after a while, she dreamed.

Ozhaguscodaywayquay was in her lodge and a White Man approached her with a cup in his hands, saying, "Poor thing, why do you punish yourself? Why do you fast? Here is food for you." The White Man had a dog at his heels who looked up into her face as if he knew her. She awoke in time to see the sun going down behind the dark forest on the opposite side of the ravine, and she entered her hut for the night, wondering about the dream. Ozhaguscodaywayquay knew that most Ojibway, men as well as women, dreamed of a special wild animal who acted as a protector of the dreamer throughout life, but she was still unsure of what her dream of the White Man and his dog meant.

During the next few days, Ozhaguscodaywayquay had the same dream over and over again until she was convinced that the Kitchi Manitou had indeed spoken to her. And, the evening after she had cut the third mark into her stick, hungry and feverish from her fast, she dreamed that she was on a high hill, very much like the one above the summer village on the point of land which stuck out into the lake. In her dream, though, the hill was entirely surrounded by water. Below, on the surface of the water, there were many birchbark canoes, each one full of Indians who were bending down and bowing to her. Then she felt light, as if she were being carried up to heaven, while beneath her the whole earth was on fire.

"All my relatives will be burned," she cried. But a voice answered, "No, they will not be destroyed; they will be saved." Ozhaguscodaywayquay realized that she was hot and crying, that her heart was pounding, and she lay panting, wondering what the last dream could have meant. The White Man and the dog were puzzling enough, but what did the Indians in their canoes, bowing to her, mean? After hours of pondering, she slept, and in the morning she gathered the broken cedar boughs and walked slowly homeward, throwing the branches on the ground before her as she went. She stepped on them, then picked up the ones behind her, only to throw them down again in front of herself, slowly making her way back to the main lodge. This, too, was part of the custom and must be done exactly right.

Her family welcomed her home, without any questions about her fast or dreams that she might have had, but for the next ten days, the grandmother allowed her to eat only a little maize boiled with a bitter herb, prepared especially for her. After the maize, for ten days she was allowed to eat only meat smoked a certain way — this food, too, prepared solely by the grandmother.

It was a warm summer, and the strawberries covered the ground with their green and red-spotted leaves before Ozhaguscodaywayquay was again allowed to eat normally with her family.

2
Sacred Union

Waubojeeg sat before his summer lodge on the sands of Chequamegon Point, facing the sun while alternately smoking his pipe filled with *kinikinick*, the tobacco of the Ojibway, and coughing. His wife and daughters were away on the mainland picking strawberries, and his sons were fishing.

Alone with his thoughts, Waubojeeg remembered that it was a day as warm as this when he had led the Ojibway warriors from these very shores against the marauding Sioux. Three hundred Ojibway had followed him. Many had been new warriors with black color on their faces and breasts. For seven days they had pushed up the Mauvais River until they had reached the upper end of the Saint Croix portage, where their scouts had surprised them with the news that the Sioux and Fox were camped on the lower end of the same portage. Behind his closed eyes, Waubojeeg saw again the narrow neck of jagged rock where the two sides had met; he again heard the men splashing in the water, saw the war clubs pounding skulls and knives entering human flesh, and heard the mixture of battle screams and cries of pain. That day the sluggish summer waters of the stream had curled red with blood; broken bodies lay everywhere. And then it had become quiet. As suddenly as the battle had begun, the enemy had fled downstream — just as the Ojibway reinforcements from Lac du Flambeau had arrived at the top of the portage trail. Among the dead had been Waubojeeg's brother. And there, too, Addick rum Maig — Deer of the Waters, Waubojeeg's best friend since childhood — had died in his arms. Only after the dead were buried had Waubojeeg realized that the blood covering his body was his own, from wounds on his breast and shoulder.

Oh, what Waubojeeg would do to have Addick back with him on the hunt! He had promised his dying friend that day beside the stream that he would marry his wife and care for his two sons, as if they were his own. And so he had. The boys were now grown men with families of their own, and although Waubojeeg had taken a second young wife some years ago, his older wife also would be cared for in his lodge until she died, as grandmother to his own children. The aging chief coughed, and the old wounds ached again, almost as they first had that summer day long ago. Waubojeeg's thoughts now turned toward the Kitchi Manitou.

"Oh Great Spirit! I believe that I will soon meet Addick in the west. Every day I feel weaker and weaker. I, Waubojeeg, who hunted each day in the winter cold,

Waubojeeg's War Song

On that day when our heroes lay low — lay low,
  On that day when our heroes lay low,
I fought by their side, and thought ere I died,
  Just vengeance to take on the foe,
  Just vengeance to take on the foe

On that day, when our chieftains lay dead — lay dead,
  On that day, when our chieftains lay dead,
I fought hand to hand, at the head of my band,
  And here, on my breast, have I bled,
  And here, on by breast, have I bled.

Our chiefs shall return no more — no more,
  Our chiefs shall return no more,
Nor their brothers of war, who can show scar for scar,
  Like women their fates shall deplore — deplore,
  Like women their fate shall deplore.

Five winters in hunting we'll spend — we'll spend,
  Five winters in hunting we'll spend,
Till our youth, grown to men, we'll to war lead again,
  And our days, like our fathers, we'll end,
  And our days, like our fathers, we'll end.

(from Schoolcraft, 1853)

must sit before the lodge like an old dog. Aaaaaaah! But I am ready. My sons are learned now in hunting and fishing, and Addick's sons help to care for their mother. My second wife is yet young and strong and can care for herself the little while until her sons are old enough to care for her. But one problem remains. My eldest daughter, Woman of the Green Glade, is now a woman, and I must choose a husband suitable for the daughter of the chief of the Ojibways of Kitchi Gami! Last fall, the White Man, Johnston, came to me and asked for her for his wife. I answered him that his customs were not our customs. I had seen white men marry our women before, and when they ceased to please their eyes, they forsook our women. I told him to go to Montreal with his furs, and if the white women there did not please him, upon his return, I would give him Ozhaguscodaywayquay.

"Johnston is a good man; he does not drink the White Man's milk, as do the French traders, and I have heard that he prays to you, Oh Great Spirit. He obtained many furs last winter, trading fairly, and even built himself a lodge of wood after his voyageurs deserted him. He lived all winter on the Island of the Golden Breasted Woodpecker without harm coming to him from the evil spirits who dwell there. But most of all, he was good to my father and his wives last winter. When the Frenchmen took Mongazida's furs and only gave him some rum in return, because he was old and weak, Johnston gave him food, even when his own supply of food was not great. Yes, he would make a worthy husband for my daughter, if he returns as he said he would. If Johnston does not come when the leaves fall from the trees, I shall give her to Buffalo — a good hunter, though a gambler.

"Great Spirit! I do not wish to leave, but I am a chief like you — although lesser by far! Still I must sometimes say words that my people like not to hear. When the winter is long and they wish to eat the seed

18

maize because their bellies have shriveled, it is I who must forbid it for the good of all the people. You have so much more power than I, and you know what is best for all of the people. So if You say that I must soon begin the Great Journey westward, so be it. I bow to You."

Waubojeeg became distracted, for over the still horizon of the great lake a small, black object appeared to be moving. As the speck steadily grew larger and became colored, Waubojeeg made out a Montreal canoe, paddled furiously by voyageurs wearing red caps. Before long, more canoes appeared in the distance, and soon the first birchbark he had sighted was being beached not far from him. The visitors were met by the barking dogs and the few children and women who were left in the village that perfect summer's day. While the voyageurs chatted and greeted the Ojibways of LaPointe, the trader John Johnston, carrying a large pack covered with canvas, made his way to the chief's lodge.

Johnston was of medium height with blue eyes and light sandy hair slightly touched with red. Despite the wide-brimmed hat he wore, his white skin had been reddened by the reflection of the brilliant sunlight on the water. Although his paddlers were dressed in buckskin trousers and blouses of homespun, he was dressed in a waistcoat and pantaloons and wore moccasins on his feet. He saluted the chief, who stood and said, impassively, "Ah, Johnston."

"Chief Waubojeeg," said the young man, "I have returned, as I promised."

This portrait of John Johnston was painted in Belfast, Ireland, by Joseph Wilson, in 1789 — a gift from John to his mother before he left for America. (Courtesy Judge Joseph H. Steere Room, Bayliss Public Library, Sault Sainte Marie, Michigan.)

"Sit down," motioned the Chief. "Let us smoke. Here I have some fresh kinikinick. Now tell me of your journey. What news do you bring from Montreal and the Sault?"

John Johnston told of the news at Montreal, of the weather on the trip out — very foggy and much rain — and of his visit at Sault Sainte Marie with Jean Baptiste Cadotte *père*, an honorable and humane gentleman who for decades had traded with the Indians at the rapids. One of the old man's sons, Jean Baptiste *fils,* was just behind even now with a brigade bound for Fond du Lac. His exploration of that area last year promised rich furs in abundance, and he would trade from there during this summer. The other son, Michel Cadotte, also intended to come back from the Sault. His wife and baby son had been baptized there, and now he wished to trade at LaPointe as he had done for six years past at various river posts. As for Johnston himself, he had traded his furs of last year for guns, balls, powder, salt, blankets, and metal kettles, and he would collect furs here again, paying the Indian trappers for them with these goods.

"And you, Sir?" he inquired of the dignified Indian. "Have you enjoyed a good winter and taken many furs?"

"This cough which you hear began in muskrat season, and does not go away, so hunting was not as enjoyable for me as in other years. Yet my sons are of an age where they are a great help to me in this endeavor, especially Wayishee, my first wife's son," explained Waubojeeg.

"And your daughters," pressed Johnston. "How do they fare this year?"

"They are healthy as chipmunks. They are picking strawberries on the mainland today."

Johnston drew a long puff on his own pipe this time. "You remember, Chief Waubojeeg, before I went to Montreal, I asked you for your daughter Ozhaguscodaywayquay. You advised me to wait until my return. I have been to Montreal, and no white woman there pleased me, so I have come to remind you of your promise."

"White Man, I remember my promise. I do not want my daughter left with children and no husband to provide deer meat for them. Now I ask a promise from you. . . . That you will marry her as the White Man marries a white woman — until your death!"

"I promise, good father," Johnston said seriously. Then, each man smoked Waubojeeg's red-bowled pipe to seal the promise, after which Johnston untied the cord binding the pack which was beside him, on the sand. He removed a long barreled gun, a carrot of tobacco, a bag of balls and one of powder, a woolen blanket, and glass beads, and laid them all before the chief.

"A brave of your nation would bring you a deer or beaver skins as a present to mark this occasion. I have only trade goods to offer you, Chief Waubojeeg. Please accept my poor gifts," said the trader.

"Your gifts will never take the place of my daughter, White Man," returned the stately father, "but I accept them as a promise that you will stay married until your death, and as a pledge that you will always care for her and your children."

By this time, the other three large canoes had landed. Each canoe was filled with voyageurs, every one of whom was more colorfully dressed than the next. Soon they, their packs, and their barrels all spilled out onto the sandy beach of Chequamegon Point amidst a noisy confusion of color and sound; there was barking and shouting, interspersed with many "Whooplas" and "Mon Dieus," and volleys from the shotguns of both Indian braves and French voyageurs. Jean Baptiste Cadotte *fils*, lifting Indian children into the air, made his way up to the lodge of Waubojeeg, whom he greeted with a hearty armclasp. Soon he was smoking and chatting with his old friend, while John Johnston sat quietly, listening to the gossip and contemplating his good fortune in winning Woman of the Green Glade.

Fresh pike caught by young boys in the narrows were soon propped against the coals of the fire on the beach, and they were now bubbling juicy and golden. When the women returned with *mokuks* full of the sweet berries from the mainland, Waubojeeg immediately summoned his second wife, who thereupon told Ozhaguscodaywayquay, her daughter, to bathe quickly and then to dress in her best white beaded deerskin dress and leggings. Woman of the Green Glade thought the special preparations were because of the voyageurs' arrival, but when she joined the lively celebration, she learned that this was her wedding feast. Already, one of the French canoemen had unwrapped his precious fiddle and was tuning up, while Jean Baptiste insisted upon opening up a keg of spirits in honor of the occasion. Waubojeeg and John were the only abstainers amongst the men who were soon singing and dancing there by the lodges. To Ozhaguscodaywayquay, it seemed but minutes before she was being carried into a canoe by her father, uncles and brothers and paddled the short distance across the sparkling dark waters to the Island of the Golden Breasted Woodpecker. Other canoes accompanied her father's; the singing and good wishes of the paddlers echoed across the lake.

Shortly, Ozhaguscodaywayquay was in the little wooden cabin Johnston had built the year before, and with many a joke and wish for long life and many children, the braves and voyageurs returned to the point on the mainland where a huge fire still illuminated the beach and the assorted merry-makers. As the singing and laughing faded away into darkness, the newlyweds were alone together for the first time. Immediately, Woman of the Green Glade fled to one corner of the dark cabin. Johnston placed his birchbark torch in the fireplace as he felt around for a candle, which he then lit and placed on his own crudely built table.

"Come, little one," he said. "I shall not harm you. Do not be afraid of me. I am your husband." His command of the Ojibway language was still unsure, and he hoped he had spoken correctly. But she huddled in the corner, her face hidden in her arms, refusing to speak or even to look at him. She was frightened, yet furious. Why had her father done such a horrible thing? Give her to a White Man? Her father, who until this night had always been so good to her! Her father knew that she had always favored Buffalo, her cousin. Oh, this White Man was so fearful in his strange clothes, with his odd smell and that hair on his face!

While Ozhaguscodaywayquay remained motionless, Johnston busied himself about the cabin, which had been empty over the summer. He unwrapped his kettles, guns, powder, calico, flour, and salt, and put them away as best as he could in the flickering candle-light. All the while, however, his heart was beating mightily against his cotton shirt.

Then he said, in English, "Well, Ozhagusco-daywayquay, are you ready to speak to me?" Silence was his only answer.

"Let us try again in the morning," he decided, and gently drew a blanket over the small buckskin-clad bundle hovering in the darkness — and then he retired, alone, to his bed across the room from her. Such was the wedding night of the twenty-nine-year-old John Johnston — born in Craig, County Antrim, in the north of Ireland — and the teenaged Ojibway maiden Ozhaguscodaywayquay born years earlier on the shores of Kitchi Gami.

3

On Island of the Golden Breasted Woodpecker

The chattering of swallows awakened Ozhaguscodaywayquay. Already warm from the summer sun, she still felt stiff. Even before she had opened her eyes, she thought, "Why do I feel so bad?" She had always loved to wake up at this time of the year because of the berry picking. Then she remembered the night before — the feasting, the rum-drinking, the singing in two and three languages, the dancing figures around the firelight, the little crooked-legged man scratching a thin stick across a hollow piece of wood to make music. Worst of all, however, she remembered that her father had given her to an old White Man to be his wife. Now that she recalled all of this, she didn't even want to open her eyes — but the room was quiet and her curiosity caused her to peek over her shoulder. She could just barely see, from this position, the White Man asleep alone on his bed. "I hate him!" she thought fiercely, as she again closed her eyes. "I will run away at my first chance. I will not be his wife!"

John was not really sleeping; actually, he was watching her from between his nearly-closed eyes. He thought, "Poor little thing. She is frightened of me. But she is a beautiful, healthy girl well raised by Waubojeeg, and she will make me a good wife if properly taught. Already her cousin Equaysayway is displaying the good training of Michel Cadotte, and I shall do as well with my little thrush. The way to bring her around to me will be like taming a wild beautiful bird. First a little food, but there will be kindness and gentleness always."

The minute that Ozhaguscodaywayquay thought that John was stirring, she again hid her head in her arms. She heard him rise and go out the door, and after a few minutes she bolted for the door, too. But he was just outside the cabin gathering wood for the fire to make his morning tea — and whistling! Again, she retreated to her corner.

For ten days, this life went on. Woman of the Green Glade stayed doubled up in her corner, her head and eyes hidden, hating and fearing her husband. For ten days, John was either in the cabin or very near it, so that she couldn't escape. He tempted her with strawberries, fresh fish, tea, and even a delicious smelling cake made with flour. But she ate little or nothing and drank water only when John was outside. In this way she felt she was proving her Indian superiority over him — Ojibway hardiness was more valuable in her eyes than his guns and kettles. Finally, one day he said gently, as he held out food to her, "Poor thing, why do you starve? Here is food for you."

Her head swam as if it had been struck a blow. John's words were those she had heard in her fasting dream! "Oh, no!" she thought in horror. "Is this White Man the guardian sent to me by the Kitchi Manitou? I refuse him! Surely, that dream was some trick played on me by the Matchi Manitou!'

But, sadly, she knew in her heart that this marriage was the will of the Great Spirit, who orders all things — even the secret dreams — for she had told no one of her special dreams, not even her dear cousin.

That very same day, John had decided to go hunting to obtain some meat for a change of diet. In the ten days, he had built a storage cabin and a root cellar. Even though he would have to leave his house to hunt, he believed that Ozhaguscodaywayquay would not know how far he had gone or how long he would be away. And, he now looked upon Ozhaguscodaywayquay as being as much a part of her corner as a barnacle is to a ship. He had waited a long time for a wife, and he certainly could wait a bit longer, if need be.

But Woman of the Green Glade had seen him take his gun, powder, and balls, and guessed that he would be gone for a long while. So shortly after his departure, she left the cabin and ran down to the lake, where she hailed some young boys fishing nearby and had them take her to the mainland in their canoe.

She was afraid to go to her father's lodge, so she went instead into the woods and built another little house of cedar boughs, just like her fasting hut. She remained there and fasted for four days, and in her torment she prayed that she might have another dream that would advise her about what to do. No dream came to her, day or night. But more and more, she thought of her cousin Equaysayway — Traveling Woman — who had married the White Man Cadotte some years before. Equaysayway ought to be back here by now from the Great Sault with her husband and babies, all of whom had gone there to be baptized, something that the Great Spirit supposedly liked white men and women to do. Equaysayway could tell her what it was like to live with a White Man. The more she thought of her cousin, the more she longed to see her again and talk to her.

So on the fourth day of her escape, she slowly returned to the summer village of her childhood. The dogs greeted her with wagging tails, and she was relieved to see that the great carved wooden owl, Kokoko, which was always perched atop Waubojeeg's lodgepole when he was in residence, was absent. This meant that her father was away, and so she freely entered his lodge and her heart was warmed for the first time in two weeks, as she spoke to her mother and the grandmother. They were too polite to ask about her last days, unless she should bring up the subject first. But Woman of the Green Glade only mentioned that her husband was away on a hunt, and they welcomed her with food, which she ate with great relish. If they wondered why she ate so much, they said nothing about it. Yes, they advised her, Traveling Woman had returned, and was indeed in the village this very day.

4

In the Middle of the Stream

Ozhaguscodaywayquay and Equaysayway, first cousins and best friends, paddled quickly along the shore of Kitchi Gami to the mouth of the Mauvais River. As they traveled, they did not speak, but once they had pushed the canoe over the bar, and into the river mouth, they went much slower — for the time had come for them to tie the tassels of some of the wild rice together to identify that part of the rice crop that would be harvested next month by their families. As they worked with the rice, they began to gossip about the changes that had taken place in the village since the last time they had seen each other.

"Buffalo is spending much time outside the lodge of Winter Star," observed Equaysayway.

"She wastes too much time," snapped Ozhaguscodaywayquay. "She will never make him a satisfactory wife."

Equaysayway wondered to herself about Ozhaguscodaywayquay's peevish reaction, and then said, "I know that you and Buffalo have been friends since you were infants, but now you are the wife of another man. Do not concern yourself with Buffalo."

With Equaysayway's remark, Ozhaguscodayway-quay ventured the thought that had plagued her these last weeks. "How can you be content with Cadotte, a White Man, for a husband?" she asked furiously.

Again, Equaysayway wondered about the sound of the question. She busied herself with cutting some rushes and laying them flat in the canoe bottom before answering. "I have never been more content in my life. Michel never lets me go without one thing that I need for myself or the babies or our lodge. The Frenchmen talk so often about 'love' and I wondered what was 'love.' But I think I love Michel and I think Michel loves me. I honor him above any man I know, except your father and mine. And Michel's father is the most good White Man I know. I hope my children will grow up to be like both grandfathers," declared Equaysayway firmly.

"But white men smell so funny, like flowers or medicine. I cannot say what they smell like," said Ozhaguscodaywayquay.

"I thought so too at first, but I no longer notice a smell," admitted Equaysayway.

"And his food. Does he ask you to cook strange food for him?" asked the new bride.

"He likes all the food I learned to cook at my mother's fire, but I learned, at his mother's house, how to cook some French dishes, and I like them as much as Michel does. I will teach them to you. Johnston will like them, too," suggested Equaysayway. "But why do you ask me all these questions when you have been a wife yourself to a White Man for over two weeks?"

Then the younger cousin confessed that she had not allowed herself to be touched by Johnston, that she had remained in the corner of the cabin the whole time, and that she had run away into the woods when the first chance to do so presented itself. She had come out expressly to see Equaysayway and to find out about her life as a wife and mother.

Equaysayway was aghast. "Ozhaguscodayway-quay, it matters not what you wish. Your father gave you to Johnston. You must go back and be his wife. If your father finds out what you have done, he will most surely beat you."

"I cannot return now. I am too ashamed of my actions. He will not want such a wife. And I am not at all sure that even now I want to go back to him. If I could do what I want, I would go back to my days before Johnston came to our land. I would go back to picking berries in the months of long and short grasses, and harvesting wild rice when the ducks fly, and making maple sugar in the month of broken snowshoes. I would be a girl without a worry again, if I could," said Ozhaguscodaywayquay.

"We have grown up, cousin. We can never go back to the days of no worries. And I would not want to. My babies are so much joy to me. Never again would I be without a child! No, motherhood gives me much more happiness than I had as a girl without troubles," Equaysayway fervently proclaimed.

Now it was Ozhaguscodaywayquay's turn to wonder. Could it be she was missing out on some truly wonderful occurrence that only a husband could bring her? "Nyah. Nyah. What am I to do?" wailed Ozhaguscodaywayquay.

"You must return to Johnston, even if he beats you and your father beats you. Come, let us hurry back. We can finish this work another day." Equaysayway believed that speed in undoing the great wrong was necessary. Besides, all of this talk about her children made her anxious to return to her own who were being cared for today by her sister. The young women turned the canoe around and maneuvered it out onto the oily summer surface of the great lake and paddled swiftly home.

Although the young friends were crossing a part of the lake, Ozhaguscodaywayquay felt as if she were in the middle of a large stream — too far from the safe bank and yet too far from the destination. All the way back to the summer village, her native word for this state of affairs — *Nawadjiwon* — echoed in her head with each stroke of the paddle.

~

Waubojeeg, on a summer hunt but only a short distance away on the mainland, had spent the night under the pine trees. The air had been warm and the ground was covered with fragrant needles, but still he had not slept well. The whole night his sleep had been troubled by a dream. It was a confused dream, but one

34

point stood out very clearly — Ozhaguscodaywayquay had run away from her husband. The chief did not interpret the dream literally, but rather he felt that it was some sort of a sign or signal. So, he left his hunting grounds without the deerskin he had been instructed to bring back by the women in his family. The animal hides so necessary for winter clothing were best when tanned in the summer, but he would continue this hunt another day. For now, he had to deal with his dream.

Waubojeeg walked overland until he came to a small bay across from his summer lodge, and there he uncovered the little canoe he had hidden in the rushes near the shore. Paddling the short remaining distance caused him to pant heavily all the while. As he entered his lodge, his first wife hurried to raise his insignia, the carved owl, on the ridgepole of the wigwam. As his eyes became accustomed to the darkness within the house, adjusting from the brilliant sunshine outside, he saw Ozhaguscodaywayquay standing quietly beside her mother.

"Why do you visit my lodge, daughter, now that you have your own?" he asked solemnly. One did not lie to the tall, powerful Waubojeeg.

"I ran away from my husband, father," she replied simply and truthfully.

"You have disgraced me!" shouted her father, singularly unused to being disgraced under any circumstances. He grabbed a stick lying near the firepit and began to beat her about the back. Ozhaguscodaywayquay did not cringe nor cry; she felt that this was just punishment for her wrongdoing. When Waubojeeg's anger was spent, he threw the stick down, and bellowed, "Now I shall return you to your rightful husband. If you run away again, I will cut off one of your ears, and if you run away a second time, I will cut off the other one!"

Grimly, he steered the suffering girl out of the lodge flap, down the beach and into his canoe, calling all the while to his wife to bring some appeasing gift for Johnston.

She ran down to his canoe with a mokuk of the first ears of maize from her garden and a newly tanned deer hide — all she could lay her hands on at that very moment.

John Johnston had returned the day before from his successful hunt, and now, in front of his cabin, he was scraping the hair from the deer hide — woman's work. He saw a canoe rapidly approaching the shoreline of his island, so he went down to the rocky beach, and his heart began to pound as he recognized the faces in the canoe. Once the birchbark was beached, Waubojeeg led the abject girl up to the trader and said, "Here is my daughter. She has disgraced our family and our nation by her behavior. Take these gifts; let them make up to you for what you have endured on her account. She will never leave you again. I, Waubojeeg, give my word!" And handing the gifts to Johnston, Waubojeeg stood proud and stately, almost as if Johnston were the one responsible for Ozhaguscodaywayquay running away.

"I was greatly saddened by her absence," the trader

said. "I welcome her back. Come, let us smoke to-gether."

Johnston handed Ozhaguscodaywayquay the maize, and commanded, "Wife, cook these ears given to us by your good father."

And Woman of the Green Glade took the basket of maize and meekly entered her own lodge to attend to her own hearth for the first time.

5

The Midewewin Society

Among the cascade of gifts which had tumbled from Johnston's blanket to Chief Waubojeeg's feet, there had been one that was hardly noticeable — a small white seashell. Falling upon the sand, the shell had been swiftly retrieved by the older man, and for several moons now he had been pondering its significance. In the traditions and stories of his people, the Ojibway called themselves Anishinabe — "the original people." The Anishinabe had migrated westward slowly from a great salt sea, led always by a sacred seashell, the *Mide Megis*. The Mide Megis had first appeared when the Anishinabe were near the great river which drains the great lakes, the river the Frenchmen called Saint Lawrence. The Mide Megis then sank into the depths until it revealed itself again on the shores of Lake Huron, then at Bow-e-ting — the place the Frenchmen called Sault Sainte Marie, located alongside the river down which the cold waters of Kitchi Gami cascade twenty-two feet as they begin their journey to the ocean. The final resting place of the wondrous shell, according to Anishinabe tradition, was the Island of the Golden Breasted Woodpecker — the site of John Johnston's cabin.

There was no doubt in Waubojeeg's mind that the recent appearance of the shell held no little significance for all of his people. Maybe this was not the Mide Megis — no White Man would have the sacred shell — but it was a white shell like the sacred shell of the Anishinabe, and it had caused him to reflect on the great journeys of his people. But why had it come to him, and in the form of a gift? What did it mean?

For two months, the ailing chief had fasted, prayed and thoughtfully smoked the sacred pipe, searching for an understanding of what was expected of him as a leader who was greatly concerned about the future of his people — thoughts inspired by the little white shell. Following his meditations and deliberations, and realizing that he was now in the final days of his own life, Waubojeeg was coming to a decision as to what he should do at this time. In his mind, it was becoming increasingly clear that the megis now represented something of a spiritual nature between the Indian and the White Man. Although he had known little about Christian beliefs, he had tried to learn more about them in conversations with Johnston, who was deeply versed in his European religion. As best as he could understand, both races believed in a powerful spirit with unlimited influence over earth and man. Both religions assured mankind of life after death. Both considered obligations to family and tribe to be of supreme importance. Only customs of marriage, hunting, and warfare seemed different, and to Waubojeeg, these were mere trappings of life and were secondary to the central question of the nature of the Kitchi Manitou and its relation to mankind. The major difference between the religions of his people and the White Man, in Waubojeeg's mind, was in the comprehension of good and evil. The Indian believed that he could call upon manitous by means of certain rituals and thereby gain some of their power for his own use. The White Man clearly separated the benevolent power of his God from an almost equal evil power of the Devil.

Waubojeeg had seen many manifestations of the power of manitous in the shaking lodges and the grand medicine rituals, and he was fully aware of the abuse of power in the traditional tale of cannibalism on the Island of the Golden Breasted Woodpecker. Many, many years ago, his tribe had lived on that island. Its location made it the perfect safe haven from bands of marauding Sioux. But Mide priests living there had resorted to unnatural acts — some said to survive harsh winters when the food was exhausted, others said to enhance their powers to the point of being invulnerable to death — this at a time so long ago that even Waubojeeg's father could not remember of the people having lived there after the evil practice had taken place. The Ojibway finally had forced the priests to stop the practice, and then simply had abandoned the island, but the priests continued to invoke ill will and misfortune on other people in order to satisfy old grudges. Yet, recently, Johnston had lived and survived on the island for an entire winter; surely, his

41

power must be greater than any Indian power to enable him to endure and overcome the presence of such a great evil.

Firm, now, in his opinion of the direction the megis was leading him, Waubojeeg was determined that the power of the Midewewin, the Grand Medicine Society of his people, should be used for the restoration of health to the people and never again for personal revenge, jealousy, and other unhappy experiences. An so, believing that the undeniable and substantial power of the Midewewin would only be utilized for unquestionable good, Waubojeeg sent out invitation sticks to all members of the Midewewin.

For four days thereafter, Waubojeeg and the other shamans fasted and spent time in the little sweatlodge of their village, purifying both their bodies and souls. Waubojeeg's thoughts during his fast turned often to the Kitchi Manitou and how he was perceived by white men and red. Both red and white admitted to the might of God manifest in thunder and lightning, to the mystery of God in death, to the love of God in birth, and to the goodness of God in the fruits of the earth. But, evil — where did that come from? Surely evil was a power, too, a power readily acknowledged in the Midewewin. The White Man held that evil comes from a devil, a Matchi Manitou, and that was that. The fact that Johnston had been the bearer of the megis was a most significant fact; to Waubojeeg, this meant that the sacred shell accepted the White Man and his ways. Always before, the Mide Megis — as it periodically appeared and disappeared — had led the Ojibway westward from the salt sea. And now, after many years of absence, a likeness of it had reappeared here, delivered from Johnston's hand to Waubojeeg's feet. Although Johnston's shell was smaller than he imagined the sacred shell to be from the stories he had heard, it clearly brought to Waubojeeg the responsibility to prepare his people to accept something of the White Man's way of life, something more than the powerful firearms and other trade goods with which they were now becoming familiar. Waubojeeg was confident that the Kitchi Manitou would speak to him and the Midewewin; it was only up to the Ojibway to interpret his words.

While Chief Waubojeeg called upon the spirits in his last, great endeavor, his family was busier than usual. His two wives and his oldest daughter had gone early to the Island of the Golden Breasted Woodpecker and were preparing a great feast of the new crop of wild rice and maize, sweet syrup obtained last March from the dripping sap of the maple trees, fresh blueberries, venison, and fish. While the feast was being readied, Waubojeeg's sons built a large and handsome *midewegun*, a medicine lodge, on the island. Branches of saplings had been forced into a succession of arches that resulted in a loaf-shaped lodge, with many green leaves woven in and out around the sides. The structure was open at the top. In the center of the great lodge was a smaller lodge, this to be used by the Midewewin for a special initiation ceremony to be held later that day.

The day of the feast was warm and the air was

still when, late that morning, the best drummer began to beat the sacred water drum. The sound of the drum carried across to the mainland, summoning the people to the island. Soon, canoes began to cross the short strait, and gradually the Midewewin and the rest of the villagers assembled on the shore of the hitherto forbidden island. Two live-cut cedar posts had been erected in the center of the inner lodge, and now Chief Waubojeeg solemnly placed his sacred rock at the base of one of the posts and a piece of buckskin filled with tobacco at the foot of the other. After lighting a fire nearby, he went outside to greet the guests.

Just beyond the sandy beach, in the shade of the leafy birches, food for the feast had been set forth by Waubojeeg's family, and the women were now busily serving everyone. No effort had been spared, and the satisfying meal lasted into the late afternoon, at which time the chief arose to speak. "Welcome, my brothers and sisters, to a new day in our pursuit of the correct path of life! For a long time we have avoided this island because of the bad events associated with it. But the evil that once was here has been conquered by the Kitchi Manitou, and his friend, the White Man Johnston. Johnston remained on this island throughout all of last winter, a harder winter than we have seen for many, many years. As a sign that the evil of this place has been cut down like a great tree in a strong windstorm, this megis has appeared."

A gasp arose from the audience as Waubojeeg flourished the white seashell before them. All recognized the object at once.

"Henceforth, our ceremonies will mark the conquest of evil by good, our sacred rites will provoke health over illness only. Today we are free to come and go, or stay here on this island as we wish. And to mark this new branch on our tree of life, today we conduct our Mide ceremonies here on this island. I invite you to join me now as the Midewewin initiates a new member into its midst." And with those words, he led his assembled people into the large lodge his sons had so recently finished building.

As daylight faded on this momentous day, young Buffalo completed his preparations to advance to the second order of the Midewewin, another step on his path of good works and guidance to others while leading an upright life himself. Then the little drums began to beat softly. Buffalo was met at the eastern door of the midewegun by four priests dressed as bears. While the assembled villagers looked on, the priests led Buffalo around the large outer lodge four times, all the while exhorting him to resist evil and temptation forever as he walked his path of life.

Meanwhile, another priest played the part of the snake and tried to obstruct Buffalo's path, forcing him to abandon the path of the bears and not relinquish evil. The sound of the drums grew within the building, while the bears shook rattles to repel the evil one. After the fourth circuit around the lodge, Chief Waubijejauk, the White Crane, leader of the highest order of the tribe's various totems, met Buffalo at the entrance of the smaller inner lodge. Solemnly, Buffalo intoned, "My eyes are shut, my ears are closed. Open my eyes; open my ears!"

Eight priests chanted their welcome, "Let our brother's eyes open and ears unblock."

Buffalo, now accompanied by his tutor, Waubojeeg, circled the inner lodge eight times to the combination of drums, rattles, and chants of the Midewewin. Finally, Buffalo sat facing the priests, at which time he was examined in detail about his knowledge of the society and required to demonstrate his new power. After he had satisfied all of the priests that he was worthy of admission to the second order of the society, Buffalo stood up. Waubojeeg pointed his *pindgigossan* — his otter skin medicine bag — at the young man and ritually shot him in the left ankle, knee, hand, and elbow with the sacred seashell, and then he swept the shell across Buffalo's belly and shot it into the young man's right ankle, knee, hand, and elbow. Now Buffalo felt the great power come over him; he could see and hear far into the future, and he could touch and sense good and evil.

In return for the gift of these powers and responsibilities, Buffalo presented shirts of the softest deerskin and wool blankets to the assembled priests. He then stood proudly as two bars were painted across his face, the stripes signifying his passage to the second order of the Midewewin. The cedar posts were taken down, after which time Buffalo departed the lodge by way of the western door.

After Buffalo's ordination ceremony, the Midewewin joined the rest of the people in the main lodge. Four drummers were seated around a large drum; they were chanting as they played, and the guests were dancing. The women shuffled along, their moccasined feet never leaving the ground, whereas the men, in beaded loincloths, lifted their legs high at the knee and hopped, first on one leg and then on the other. The children joined in the dance, too, mimicking the adults. After some time, Waubojeeg entered the center of the circle of dancers, and slowly, one by one, the dancers moved to the sides of the lodge and took seats alongside those who were not dancing. The lodge was now dark, except for the flickering fire reflecting off of the feet of the elderly chieftain. Ozhaguscodaywayquay watched proudly as her father stood in the midst of his people.

Old yet dignified, Waubojeeg inhaled from his long redstone pipe, then exhaled a single puff of smoke — directing it skyward toward the Kitchi Manitou with an offer of thanksgiving for all of his creations. The second whiff of smoke was aimed at the earth, which sustains life. Successive puffs were sent first to the east, from whence each new day dawned; to the west, the Land of the Souls; to the north, in recognition of the laws that, though hard, are necessary to govern life; and finally, to the south, with gratitude for the eternal cycle of growth.

Next, Waubojeeg, fabled storyteller of the Anishinabe, recounted for the last time the sacred story of his people. He recalled how the Anishinabe had lived on the shores of a great salt lake from whence a small sea shell had emerged and hovered over them for a long time, frightening the people and puzzling the medicine men. He reminded them how the people finally had dismantled their lodges and followed the megis westward, the megis sometimes floating in the sky above them, then at other times disappearing beneath the water of the lakes and rivers along their route. But finally, Waubojeeg told them, the megis had settled right here on the very shore upon which they were gathered this very night, and that they should always remember and be grateful for the many things that their grandmothers and grandfathers had done for them. Then, Waubojeeg reached into his pindgigossan and brought forth the seashell he had obtained from Johnston. He held it high in the faint and quivering light of the bonfire and proclaimed that the megis had again appeared and that this reappearance was meant to improve the condition of all the people. He welcomed any who were ill to come forward and be healed.

Slowly, an old woman came forward, and then others followed to try this wondrous medicine. Waubojeeg ritually shot each of them with his pindgigossan, and each in turn fell to the ground at his feet, still and dead-like. Then he shot the afflicted person again, and as the white megis fell from his medicine bag to the ground, the once-infirm person sprang up, laughing and joking with those nearby, apparently healed.

Amid the general hilarity, the drumming began again and soon the dancers were going round and round the lodge, joined now by even the elderly and once-crippled who had received the favor of healing. This part of the ceremony lasted until dawn, and it was

---

Waubojeeg's Death Song

My friends when my spirit is fled — is fled
  My friends when my spirit is fled,
Ah, put me not bound, in the dark and cold ground,
  Where light shall no longer be shed — be shed,
  Where day-light no more shall be shed.

But lay me up scaffolded high — all high,
  Chiefs lay me up scaffolded high,
Where my tribe shall still say, as they point to my clay,
  He ne'er from the foe sought to fly — to fly,
  He ne'er from the foe sought to fly.

And children, who play on the shore — the shore,
  And children who play on the shore,
As the war dance they beat, my name shall repeat,
  And the fate of their chieftain deplore — deplore,
  And the fate of their chieftain deplore.

(from Schoolcraft, 1853)

greatly enjoyed by all of the guests. But Waubojeeg, exhausted and coughing blood, had retired to the side of the lodge when the dancing resumed. He was glad that the chants and the drumming obscured the sounds of his choking, for he wished his wives and children to enjoy themselves. He himself had always danced at every feast until this one, but as this night passed, he lay in the dark, listening to all of the sounds and knowing it would be the last time he would ever hear them in this life. All had gone as he had expected, save for his own power; it had healed everyone but himself.

49

Instead, he was enveloped in a damp, clammy sweat, punctuated by great fits of coughing which finally became so pronounced that Ozhaguscodaywayquay came running to his side. Alarmed by the blood on his lips and nose, she took his head onto her lap, oblivious to the red spots all over her white buckskin wedding dress.

6

It Is Permitted

C hief Waubijejauk — face painted, head adorned with feathers, and dressed in his best white fringed buckskin clothing — arose from the cluster of dark heads and stood above the long birchbark-covered bundle resting on the floor of the lodge. He spoke solemnly and distinctly.

"Brothers and Sisters, we are gathered today to bid farewell to a great chieftain of our nation. Waubojeeg wore the black feather from childhood. His uncle, the Sioux chief Wabasha, prophesied, when eight-year-old Waubojeeg struck him with a toy warclub, that this would be a great warrior. And we all know well how Waubojeeg united all of the Ojibway that memorable summer so long ago, and how he led us up the Mauvais River to the Saint Croix, where on the cliffs we met the Sioux. There were many more of them than there were of us. But we fought so well that the enemy either died from our blows or fell over the waterfalls there on that river. So terrible was this battle, that the enemy has never since invaded our hunting grounds! Waubojeeg himself sustained three bad wounds from this battle, and he will always be remembered among our people for this great deed.

"Oh Great Spirit! Receive this great story-teller, Waubojeeg! Your winters will be enriched by him, as ours will be impoverished. A mighty hunter, too, was this chief. Many a deer we stalked together, many a winter's night we slept together on the snow! He cared well for his family; starvation never came into his lodge. After the battle of the Saint Croix, he took the wife of his friend who died in that battle and raised their two sons as his own. Now he has a good wife and six children of his own, and still the first wife is cared for in his lodge. Waubojeeg, always ready to give good advice to his brother, always fair in dealing with the white trader, the whole Ojibway nation, from the north where Nanabujou lives to the Grand Sault, will grieve for the loss of you, our great chieftain who never drank the White Man's milk!"

At this point, Waubijejauk looked at Waubojeeg's mourning wives and the assembled children. Ozhaguscodaywayquay's eyes met his. As befitted the daughter of such a great chief, she held her head high and refused to cry in view of her relatives and friends.

Waubijejauk went on. "But let us be happy and not show grief. Waubojeeg has only passed to the land beyond which awaits all of us, and surely we will follow him soon and be united again."

Waubijejauk then addressed the wives directly. "Mothers, do not be idle; labor helps one to forget grief.

Labor will be of comfort to you and it will preserve the good habits that your husband fostered. Rise with the sun; retire with the sunset. Kitchi Manitou is always with us all."

At the conclusion of Waubijejauk's oration, the body of Waubojeeg, covered with mats of birchbark, bound and laced with root twine, *wigub*, was raised by his friends and passed through an opening on the east side of the lodge to others, waiting on the outside, who now took up his remains. Slowly, moving along a path now covered with dry leaves that crackled and scattered with each footstep, they carried him to his final resting place well inland from the summer village on the lake. His body was followed by the tribal drummer, who wailed and beat the instrument woefully. Behind the drummer marched family and friends, chieftains, Mide priests and even, at the end of the procession, the village dogs. The day was gray, and the wind was chilly as it gusted around the blanket-sheathed mourners. Wayishee, one of the sons of Waubojeeg's first wife, carried the new gun which John Johnston had given the chief, and Waubojeeg's younger wife brought a bowl of newly harvested wild rice boiled with maple sugar and venison — the dead man's favorite dish. Ozhaguscodaywayquay walked beside her mother, carefully holding her father's warclub against her burgeoning belly as if trying to impart some of its strength to the tiny body growing within her. She thought about the last four days and was satisfied. Everything had been done properly, even magnificently, according to custom. But that was the way a chief should depart —

not like a dog, but grandly, with his prized possessions beside him for the dangerous trip to the Land of Souls, after a fine feast for all the honored guests.

Earlier, Ozhaguscodaywayquay had helped to wrap her father in the birchbark matting and had woven a colorful scarf into the wigub. Johnston had given her the scarf, and she had wanted some part of her to go with Waubojeeg. Now, as she reflected, she felt as if there had been a certain beauty to her father's death — he had merely grown weaker and weaker until finally reaching the end — and to the ceremonies conducted by the Midewewin and her uncle Waubijejauk. "All life is a gift from the Great Manitou," she thought, recalling Waubijejauk's words, "and if my father always dignified that gift in his own life, so we must dignify his departure from it." Even now she was preparing for the Kitchi Manitou's gift of new life by embroidering the whitened deerskin with porcupine quills and tiny glass beads. This garment would be laced onto the *tikinagan* that would hold her baby. She was ready to welcome the new life within her with the same strength that she was now using to bid farewell to the old life before her.

The procession moved far into the forest. With much effort, the body of Waubojeeg was raised up to a scaffold that had been erected halfway up a large elm tree, where the branches started to reach outward. His gun and rice bowl were placed beside him, gifts that would aid him on his trip westward. All gathered at the foot of the tree as the medicine man began to speak.

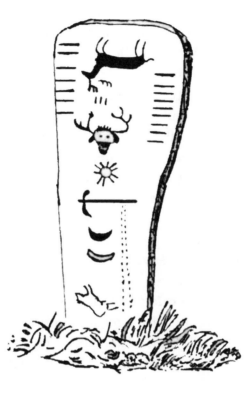

Although Waubojeeg instructed that his remains be left on the burial scaffold and not buried, he apparently did have a grave post commemorating his life. "He was of the family or clan of the addik, or American reindeer. This fact is symbolized by the figure of the deer. The reverse position denotes death. His own personal name, which was the White Fisher, is not noticed. The seven transverse marks on the left denote that he had led seven war parties. The three perpendicular lines below the totem, represent three wounds received in battle. The figure of a moose's head, relates to a desperate conflict with an enraged animal of this kind. The symbols of the arrow and pipe, are drawn to indicate his influence in war and peace" (from Schoolcraft, 1851–1857, volume 1).

"Waubojeeg, do not cast regretful glances upon your relatives and friends. You have finished all earthly acts; do not be disturbed by our tears. In a short time, we, too, must go to the setting sun." Waubojeeg's first wife begged to be the one to remain with him for four days to keep a vigil fire going near the scaffold, and since his second wife had children who were still quite young, she granted the request.

The sorrowful mourners turned and began retracing their steps to the winter encampment near the waters which oozed out of the ground all year long. Ozhaguscodaywayquay, walking beside her mother, thought, "Now I can leave my home, as Johnston wishes me to do. My father's death has spoken to me. My mother will be cared for by Wayishee; he has promised to do so. When the birds return, Johnston and I and the little one will go to the Sault. My father was so correct to give me to Johnston — he is such a good and gentle man. My father was always right. How he beat me that day I ran away!" Her behavior on that occasion seemed to her as if it had happened years ago instead of just a few months before. It almost seemed that she couldn't remember when she had not been married to John. The babe within her kicked mightily, and she thought again, as she had done often these days, how happy she would be when the child was born. Johnston wished for a boy, but she, knowing how much help she would need around the cabin with more children to come, wished for a girl. But she wished secretly, for she honored the pride that a son would give Johnston.

Johnston wanted to move to the Sault where he could open a trading post. Michel Cadotte and Equaysayway had visited the Sault, but while there they missed their home on Kitchi Gami so much that they returned to LaPointe. The plan was for Michel to take over Johnston's cabin on the island and for Johnston to go to the Sault where Michel's father, Jean Baptiste, had long been a trader. Jean Baptiste was getting old and wished to give up the business, but his sons preferred to be on the shores of Kitchi Gami — Jean Baptiste *fils* at Fond du Lac and Michel here at the Island of the Golden Breasted Woodpecker. The elder Cadotte would assist Johnston in getting started and both families would cooperate as independent traders competing against the great North West Company. Ozhaguscodaywayquay had been reluctant to leave her family, but the Ojibway have a word for fate — *inaendaugwut*, it is permitted — which means that events are permitted by forces outside of man himself. And so Ozhaguscodaywayquay felt that this major loss — the death of her father — was a sign that her departure for the Sault was not only permitted; indeed, it was being urged upon her by some great and mysterious force.

Waubojeeg's warclub was to have been placed with his body on the burial platform, but at the last moment Ozhaguscodaywayquay refused to give it up. She wanted to take this treasured object to the Sault to remind her of her former life, her beloved father, and of all the fond experiences of her life among her people. She looked at the familiar forest around her, thinking that

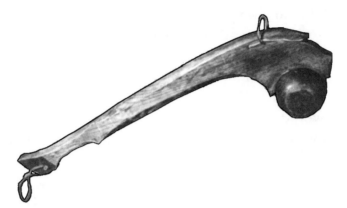

Waubojeeg's warclub is now in the collections of Le Sault de Sainte Marie Historical Society, Sault Sainte Marie, Michigan. (Photograph by Jack Soetebier.)

it possibly might be the last time she would ever see it — the bare-branched trees; the mounds of tan, dry, curled leaves beneath them; and the scattered clusters of somber evergreens, now almost black in the pale light of late autumn.

The winter village came into sight. The lodges, surrounded by branches piled high, were ready for the never-ending winter fires. Ozhaguscodaywayquay's eyes searched for her father's lodge — and there it stood, ridgepole bare, Waubojeeg's owl no longer turning in the wind.

7

Kitchi Gami

Ozhaguscodaywayquay quietly slipped a little kinickinick and grains of *manomin,* wild rice, onto the waters of the lake as their Montreal canoe glided through the silky waves. Here there was much manitou, and when near this place the Ojibway always made offerings to the god of the water, Misshipeshu, and the rock spirits. She didn't want Johnston to see her do this — he called it superstition — but with the mighty waves and winds of Kitchi Gami ever ready to burst into fury at a moment's notice, she wished to take no chances on inciting the wrath of anybody's god while her precious baby boy — Lewis Saurin, namesake of the Attorney General of Ireland — was aboard. Even so, she knew full well that Johnston and the voyageurs prayed often to various saints, and in her heart she believed them all to be the same as the Ojibway spirits — only with different names, some French and some English.

To the left of Ozhaguscodaywayquay stretched the

limitless gray blue waters of Kitchi Gami, and close on her right side were immense and strange rock formations. From where she sat these rocks looked like the hind end of a huge, fat, buff-colored dog, and they could have easily maneuvered the forty-foot-long canoe between the legs of the dog. The mainland, as far as the eye could see, was an exposed rocky cliff made up of various colored layers. The caves and towers came right to the water's edge and, John assured her, they looked like the houses and castles of Montreal. A small waterfall cascaded into sight, but nowhere on this strange shore was there room for their large party of several canoes to land if the weather should worsen and the winds come up, as could happen so quickly.

"That one looks like the doorway to Saint Anne's," shouted one of the voyageurs as they paused to rest and smoke. "And that one is the church itself!" exclaimed another. Silently, all prayed that the good weather would hold until they had rounded the point of land far ahead; it would be the only safe place at which to put ashore for many, many miles. Ozhaguscodaywayquay opened her embroidered deerskin pouch and took out some hazelnuts and lumps of maple sugar which she then passed around. This snack would give strength to everyone for the remainder of the day's work, and it also made her feel a little useful, too, since — although she could paddle as well as a man — John would not allow her to do so. He said that she must care for their son, but she thought the real reason he would not let her paddle was because he wanted the voyageurs to have as much respect for her as they had for white women. So she spent her time nursing the baby, whittling toys for him, and, when the lake was calm, even stitching new moccasins for John. Now and again, she merely held the sleeping child and looked with curiosity and wonder at the landscape through which they were passing.

Near her father's fire she had heard of these spectacular lands from many visitors, both red and white, but this was the first time she had seen them with her own eyes. At one point she found herself thinking, "How is it that the White Man cannot see the gods of the earth as clearly as our people can? Surely Kitchi Manitou is power, and where is there more power than in the fury of the great lake when it is angry? And the waves — their power can overturn even these heavily laden canoes and carry away whole pieces of land, as they have assuredly done on these shores! And the power that appears in the sky when the heavens' gods are angry and the thunderbirds send flashes of light to earth and pound their thunder drums. Surely that is power. It is so easy to believe in such gods! But, 'No,' Johnston says, there is but one God and all power is his. Well, what is the difference? We must leave kinickinick and manomin for the gods when we undertake any great thing, whether there be one or many of them.

"And if there is but one God, how does He feel about the traders taking away so many little animals of the forest? The guns received in trade for the animal skins have been good for the hunters. Since the traders came, there has always been enough deer meat

61

for even the hardest winter, unlike the starvation that used to be frequent in the winter lodges. But the guns are used to harm other men, too. My cousins and older brothers went off to battle with the Sioux in the summers with guns. My marrying a White Man might prevent our son from having to go on the warpath. Well, a gun received in trade is like anything else — it can be used for good or bad, depending upon the wishes of the person using it."

Tired from dwelling on concerns about the future and questions for which there were no final answers, Ozhaguscodaywayquay sighed and settled down amongst the bales of fur. Even though the spring air was cool, the sun was warm and so were the furs, and soon both she and her babe were deeply asleep.

The weather had been fair so far. With only gentle west winds, the canoes were often propelled by the wind, allowing the voyageurs to rest. They traveled until after dark each night, and began the next day's journey before dawn. The men coughed and made queer noises while loading their cargo back into the canoes, and then — after a bowl of hot tea and leftovers from the previous night's supper — they were in the canoes and moving by first light. Often a pause and a pipe were called for as the sun broke over the horizon ahead of them. The beautiful sunrises over the lake were feasts for Ozhaguscodaywayquay's eyes as she nursed Lewis Saurin for the first time each day — a time she loved because it gave her an excuse to hold him instead of lacing him into the tikinagan. Her stomach muscles tightened into a hard knot and hurt a little as he sucked, still she gloried in this activity whilst feelings of gratitude to Johnston for making her a mother filled her heart. Equaysayway had been correct; never again could she imagine her life without a child in it.

After Lewis had been fed and attended to, he would fall asleep, lulled into comfort by the motion of the boat or the songs his mother would sing. Often, the Frenchmen too would sing, celebrating the joy of being alive and strong and able to exist in this invigorating world where the natural phenomena of wind and waves, cold and wet, daily tested their manhood. The men loved having a baby around, too. They sang quietly when he slept, and they took turns holding him in their arms as they sat around the campfire at night while his mother helped the cook prepare the evening meal. The cook would make the usual soup of dried peas and fat, but Ozhaguscodaywayquay would add a fish baked golden against the hot coals of the fire or wild rice cooked with maple sugar. One day John had shot some mallards, and that night the travelers enjoyed fowl baked Indian fashion — tied by their necks on a stick over the hot fire, and turned slowly until they were juicy and brown.

After eating, the men would retire to sleep beneath the overturned canoes, surrounded by a fortune in the pelts of mink, marten, fox, ermine, muskrat and beaver. Ozhaguscodaywayquay, John, and baby Lewis slept under a bear skin, a warm nest for this time of year when frost still covered the trees and boulders along the shore each morning.

Several days into the journey, and only two days

before they would reach the Sault, if the weather continued fair, John lit his tobacco with a flint and gazed at Ozhaguscodaywayquay nestled in her luxurious nest of fur bales. Like a little brown and black bird, she cuddled the baby under her wing. John reflected on how lucky he had been to gain her for a wife. He admitted to himself that his reason for asking Waubojeeg to let her become his wife had been to secure trade with the Ojibway; as an independent trader not allied with one of the big companies, he had had to consider such an approach in this wilderness with its own set of relentless laws. Still, day by day, he had come to respect and love her inordinately. He greatly admired her absolute constant industry. She was always busy; if not with the baby, then she was sewing skins or whittling some bowl or tool. The infant was almost unobtrusive, far different than would be the case traveling with a white woman and child. When Lewis needed feeding, Ozhaguscodaywayquay quietly attended to the task, and when the diaper needed to be changed she would dispose of the used moss in the lake and apply fresh moss from the supply she constantly replenished. She knew about medicinal herbs and plants, and, in short, understood how to utilize every bit of this land that, to most Europeans, appeared hostile and inhospitable. Ozhaguscodaywayquay was not only at home in it; she relished every nuance of it. Just the night before, she had described the brilliant *aurora borealis*, shining and darting across the sky, as the graceful headdresses of Ojibway spirits dancing in heaven. Those powerful flashes had brought south winds this day, which prompted the voyageurs to put up their canvas sails; to their laughing and cheering, the boat skimmed over the swells, past the evergreen-shrouded shores, to the point of the whitefish.

Once at the Sault, John Johnston quickly built a cabin south of the Saint Marys River next to the home of Jean Baptiste Cadotte. John realized that a great commercial opportunity existed here. The North West Company operated a fort, or post, on the north side of the rapids, but he would take over Jean Baptiste's trad-

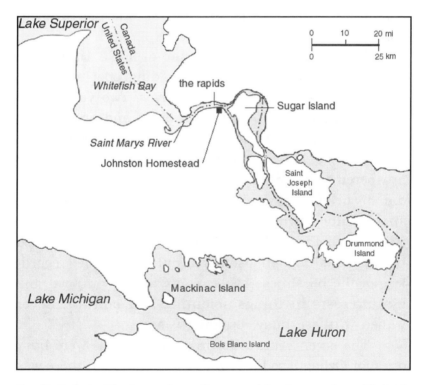

Sault Sainte Marie and environs, with the modern United States - Canada boundary shown.

ing post on the south side and do business with the independent traders like the Cadotte brothers. After all, everyone who traveled to or from Lake Superior, or between the land north and south of the river, had to pass through the Sault. He would be strategically well located to provide products and services to travelers and traders alike who were moving through the area. Another tremendous asset was the fact that the Ojibway people who had lived in this area for many years were related to Waubojeeg's people, and as a result Ozhaguscodaywayquay was as greatly respected here as the daughter of a great chief as she had been at Chequamegon.

It was during the summer of 1793 that John Johnston built his home and trading post along the south bank of the Saint Marys River. Two years later, the Johnston's son George was born, and on January 31, 1800, the first girl, Jane, joined her brothers in the sturdy cabin on the river bank. John's business prospered throughout the next six years, and not only did he become a wealthy man, he was also well respected for always being helpful to any person in trouble, whether Indian or White Man. John maintained his religious and philosophical outlook on life, regardless of the harshness of its reality at this outpost, and his interests in things scientific and cultural never waned in these busy, building years.

The seven years following her marriage were busy ones for Ozhaguscodaywayquay too. Although there was always an Ojibway niece or cousin to help in the house with cooking and cleaning, only she could nurse the babies as they arrived. And as time consuming as this job was, there was none she enjoyed more. Ozhaguscodaywayquay herself had been raised tightly strapped to the tikinagan, and so her mother had taught her that she should do the same with her children, but she changed her view of this practice as she came into contact with the French women at the Sault and saw how much they held and cuddled their babies. Although she kept the tikinagan ready for each of her children as they came along, she increasingly kept each one out of it for longer and longer periods of time, usually by extending the freedom associated with nursing time.

As the years went on, more and more, Ozhaguscodaywayquay thought of herself as a bridge between

Sault Sainte Marie in 1821. This view of the rapids from the south side of the Saint Marys River would have been from near the Johnston homestead. Buildings of the North West Company are on the opposite bank. (Courtesy Judge Joseph H. Steere Room, Bayliss Public Library, Sault Sainte Marie, Michigan.)

the Ojibways and the whites, bringing the knowledge of one to the other. Increasingly, she realized that both cultures had appealing features and strong qualities, yet neither had all the answers to life and living. And so she became determined to take the good of the White Man's ways, such as the wooden lodges, iron kettles, soap, woolen socks and, yes, even his Christianity, to the Indians. At the same time, she gave the White Man the Indian's knowledge of the forests, the lakes, the plants and animals, and their sense of oneness with all of nature. Often, when she was picking berries or doing some other repetitive chore, her youthful dream would return to her, and she thought with awe how prophetic it had been — Johnston had offered her food, and her intercessions on behalf of her relatives to the White Man had made her honored amongst her people. But what of the little dog whose eyes had gazed with such familiarity into her own? At last, she decided that the dog had represented a friend, and Equaysayway was the friend who had convinced her to return to Johnston. Satisfied that all the pieces fit together, she thanked the Kitchi Manitou more than once for the graceful unfolding of her life.

As Ozhaguscodaywayquay's exceptional life progressed, her maiden name was used less and less. To her children she became known as Neengay, "my mother," and to John she became Susan. John confided that Susan sounded a little like Ozhaguscodaywayquay and it was much easier for white men to pronounce and certainly it was much easier to write in his letters home to Ireland.

8

The Great Divide

John Johnston, now forty-seven, surveyed himself in the mirror, the first one he had seen in many years. Tall, with small deep-set eyes, his blond hair, receding slightly, was tied back with a ribbon. Yes, he looked the part of an Irish gentleman in his velvet waistcoat and breeches. But the white stockings were too tight for his liking, and the buckled shoes were not nearly as comfortable as the moccasins he had been wearing for the past nineteen years. Over the many years that had passed since Susan and he had come to the Sault, he had become known among the French with whom he worked and lived as "John Johnston, Irish Indian." He was proud of the "Irish" part of the appellation, and he was pleased that two decades in the wilderness had not erased the bearing of an Irish gentleman.

After all, he had left Ireland with many unhappy feelings a generation ago. The Lord of Donegal had repudiated the promise made by his grandfather that the Johnston family should always manage the Belfast city waterworks — a facility that had been constructed by John's grandfather William, who was known by the nickname of "Pipewater Johnston." John had been manager of the waterworks, but after only three years of the young man's stewardship, the Lord had turned the system over to the city of Belfast. John, embarrassed by this turn of events, thereupon had departed for the port of New York.

But now, during this winter of 1809, self assured, confident, and mature, John Johnston had returned to Craig, the family's ancestral home. His mother had died five years before and he had come home to help with the affairs of the estate. Often in the dark and cold woods, he had recalled the humiliation he felt when he had been removed from his post at the waterworks, and he had vowed that he would gain the wealth of the woodlands and return to Ireland in better circumstances than when he had left. And so he had! There were few items in the shops which he could not afford, if he desired them. As he stood there before the mirror, he again toyed with the idea of returning to Craig to live. Now, he could pursue the life of an Irish country gentleman. His connections at the Sault would continue to send furs to him here in Ireland, where they would command a fine price. And his five children could have a good education here. Jane, already a beautiful child, would be well placed socially and could have a beautiful marriage. But when he tried to fit Susan into this culture of calling cards, corsets, curls, mutton, and carriages, it did not accommodate her well. He made a wry face.

As he tied the silk cravat with inexperienced hands, his thoughts turned to his daughter Jane, who always had been a little on the frail side and clearly was not experiencing good health at this time. She had come to Ireland with him and had been staying here at the home of his favorite sister, Jane, who lived in County Wexford in southern Ireland. Jane had at first attributed her namesake's upset stomach to the vast difference in the food between that of the Sault and Ireland. But now that he and young Jane had been in Ireland for a month, and she was progressively growing thinner and weaker, John was forced to conclude that at least part of her suffering was due to plain old-fashioned homesickness.

Oh yes, young Jane played with other children, she loved the new clothes made for her by Jane's sempstress, and — because John himself had grounded her well in reading and composition back home — she was able to keep up with the tutor. She did especially well in piano instruction. Yet, she missed her loving, easy-going, cheerful mother and her brothers and sisters: Lewis, George, Eliza, and the new baby, Charlotte, the "wild rose," now nearly four years old. And, she missed other things about home as well — the blueberry picking which took place in the fall; the sledding in the snow, such an important part of her winter; the storytelling before the roaring fireplace during those long winter nights. She was already looking forward to spring and the first strawberries. How could John tell her that here in County Wexford the servants picked the berries, and that she could eat them

Jane Johnston, date of photograph unknown. (Courtesy Johnston Family Papers, Bentley Historical Library, University of Michigan, Ann Arbor, Michigan.)

in a bowl covered with rich cream when she would rather splash through the wet morning grass and seek them out herself, as she had always done with her mother?

The sound of voices in the room below told John that his sister's holiday dinner was getting underway, and that he had better finish dressing, pick up his daughter, and join the guests. When they reached the wainscoted room, it had already been warmed by the huge logs burning in the fireplace and a multitude of candles burning in the chandeliers. He made his way slowly through the crowd, greeting those whom he had already met following his arrival here at Jane's and being introduced to other of her neighbors and friends. Young Jane clung shyly to his side, eyes wide and curious. Vicar McNeil, a relative of his mother's, induced John to sit down with him over their glasses of sherry.

"Enchanting child, your Jane," the portly gentleman exclaimed. "Such fragile beauty, such manners, one would never suspect that her mother had come from such savage people as the Indians."

Johnston winced at this statement. "Her mother is a highly respected member of a great nation, the daughter of a renowned chieftain named Waubojeeg. And, the entire Ojibway nation is, to an unusual degree, polite. Indeed, I generally have found Indians of all tribes to be extremely gentle as long as we do them no harm. The term 'savage' seems only to apply when they are fighting each other or Europeans who intrude on their hunting and fishing territories," he answered, thinking to himself that no Ojibway would refer to a child's mother with an uncomplimentary term in the child's presence.

"Extraordinary!" shouted the vicar. "And she is a lovely color, too. Much lighter of skin than I would have thought possible in just one generation of mixture with white blood, if you'll pardon my saying so."

"Her grandfather was quite light of skin," John returned mildly. "In fact, Sir, his name in Ojibway means 'White Fisher' — a fisher is a furbearing animal of exceedingly fine quality. The adjective 'white' is of great distinction among the Indian. The Ojibway believe that long ago the Great Spirit sent them messengers with gifts of a white hare skin and the feathers of a white-headed eagle in a white otter skin. These items proved to be goodly medicines which healed them; henceforth, white is their color of life and is sacred to them."

"How difficult it must be for you, Sir, to live in primitive wilderness, cut off from society of your own kind and lacking all amenities, periodicals, the consolation of religion. Do you find it so?" lamented the vicar, sipping sherry from his cut-glass goblet.

"I must confess," said Johnston, "that I do miss ready access to the latest books and journals, but they finally arrive each spring aboard the canoes from Montreal. They are only a little bit out of date when they reach me, which hardly matters to us in our remote corner. For all of the announcements of deaths, battles, triumphs, and scandals, what can we do about them anyway, eh? Whether we learn of them timely or late? And as for investigations and experiments into electricity, magnetism, and all of earth science, they will last and are valid forever more, so timeliness is of no consequence. These, sir, are my main interests — indeed, my passions."

"And your wife?" inquired the cleric. "Judging by your lovely little daughter, I venture to say she must be a very pretty woman."

"I think she is quite lovely," John replied honestly. "She is taller than you and rather full-size now after having had five children, although when we married she was quite slim. She has long straight hair which is pulled into a tail or twist, her skin is brown, and she is very beautiful in her manner of treating every person with honest friendliness, whether they be man or woman, young or old, dark or light skinned."

"What a charming description! And what do you think she is doing at this very moment?" pursued McNeil.

John relished his role of raconteur, and went on with a reflection upon what life at his home at the Sault probably was like at this very time. "At this season, it is many degrees below the temperature when water freezes, and the Grand Sault, or rapids, is a mass of crystal whorls as beautiful as any Waterford decanter. Along the shores of the Saint Marys River, the winter blanket of purest white snow by now is, oh, at least up to my waist. In places where the wind blows without impediment, the snow is sculptured into fantastic and curious shapes, often looking like the French pastries Jane so dearly loves in the baker shops here.

The stars cover every inch of the inky black sky, and the air is clear and pure and cold beyond belief. Most likely, an old Ojibway storyteller, Bird in Eternal Flight, has come to our home and, with a wealth of descriptive movements, is relating ancient legends to my family and servants before a fire of birchen logs in the stone fireplace which I myself built. My wife will be sitting in a rocking chair, with a child cuddled up against her, and the wind outside will be howling and shaking the doors and windows."

Then, all at once, as if awakening from a dream, he thought to himself, "My God, what am I doing here in this over-heated room with all of these strangers?"

He immediately excused himself on the pretext of seeing to it that Jane got to bed, since her health was so precarious these days. But he knew that night, at that moment, that he had crossed a divide and realized that he was now more "Indian" than "Irish." He could hardly wait to return to Susan, the deep and silent forest, and the Sault — the awesome breast of Kitchi Gami. From this moment on, he never again entertained the idea of returning to Ireland to live, and the very next day he began to purchase supplies and gifts in preparation for the long journey home.

9
Bow-e-Ting

W hen Johnston described for vicar McNeil what he thought Susan might have been doing at that exact moment, taking into account the difference in time between Craig and the Sault, he was remarkably accurate. The cold, the snow, the starlit sky and even his own fireside were, that December night, just as he had described them — with but one exception. It was not an old Ojibway storyteller who sat before the aromatic, crackling fire that night.

No. It was Shingaba Wossin, the Image Stone, strong of arm and firm of thigh, at the height of his manhood who was there, and he was telling the story of Shingebis, the duck who outwitted the winter through his perseverance. No matter how hard the Winter Wind tried, the duck found food and remained cheerful. The outcome of the story was that the canny and sturdy duck simply invited the fierce North Wind into his lodge, and then made such a hot fire that the winter was forced to retreat. The Ojibway loved this story, ancient as it was. They likened themselves to the duck and the character of winter to the relentless invasion of the White Man. Shingaba Wossin enacted the tale with great flourishes, and the little children laughed and giggled at his antics. Susan smiled, too, from her chair nearest the fire. She was rocking her youngest, Charlotte, who had a slightly stuffy nose and fussed from time to time. Susan was happy that Shingaba Wossin entertained, taught, and amused her children and servants, but to herself she thought that he was not nearly as good a storyteller as her father had been!

Still there was a special bond between herself and Shingaba Wossin. Each Ojibway band had access to some special property. Some Ojibway at the western end of Kitchi Gami knew where to find copper; others in the south obtained salt or pipestone. Her tribe lived on Kitchi Gami where strange little gray or

Image stones from the upper Great Lakes region (from Schoolcraft, 1853).

tan colored rocks which occurred in fanciful shapes were found. One might look like a baby, others like a man's head, a toe, a moccasin, a perfectly round ball, or a whole man with arms and a head. These were called "image stones." Susan had brought a bagful of them with her to the Sault, and when she had met Chief Image Stone fifteen years ago she gave some of the stones to him. He had never before seen so many of the little rocks for which he had been named and, as a result, there had developed a special friendship between the two. Shingaba Wossin had come to Susan's house this night to be sure that all was well with her and her family in the absence of her husband. He could see that she was well provided for — the woodpile beside the house was still stacked high and contained enough wood to last until the month of maple sugar, at least. All inside were fat and well-fed. Susan asked only about his hunting and trapping; she knew how to introduce the subject if she had a need of any kind.

When Shingaba Wossin finished the story, Susan offered tea and a kind of pancake to all and, while they were eating, Shingaba Wossin thought that if Johnston did not return from the White Man's world, either by accident or design, he would ask this woman to be his wife. His wife had died within the past year, and he needed companionship. Susan chatted cheerfully as she fed her young children and her visitor. It was good of Image Stone to come to see if she needed help, and she plainly showed her gratitude by extending him her hospitality.

After Shingaba Wossin had gone out into the cold,

still night, wrapped in his blanket and looking so much like her father, and after all of her children were in bed, she went alone to her bedroom under the eaves and snuggled under the bear fur covering that she had brought all the way from LaPointe — it had been a wedding gift from her father. Then she thought, "Why did I not let Shingaba Wossin stay the night? How do I know that Johnston will ever return?" In the dark room, it seemed as if he had been gone forever. At this thought, a stab of pain went through her heart. "Never to see Jane again? No, no! He couldn't do that! Not beautiful Jane — Obahbahm-Wawa-Geshagoquay, The Sound the Stars Make Rushing Through the Sky. But John wouldn't stay away. He gave me his word that he would return; he has always kept his word before."

But, as much as she desired to see her eldest daughter, more like a sister to her than a child, another pain assailed her, too — the desire to lie beside a strong healthy man was almost overwhelming. The girl who had been frightened of John Johnston so many years ago on the Island of the Golden Breasted Woodpecker had grown into a loving woman and mother who longed for her husband more than she had ever imagined possible.

The weather of that spring of 1810 was not the most favorable for crossing the Atlantic Ocean, but John had determined that he and Jane would take an early ship for the New World, so eager were they both to return home. In April, they went to England where John had business to conduct, and then they set sail from Liverpool for America in June.

John's books and other publications — which included some of the classics, issues of *The Beaver* and the new humor journal *Punch*, and many British newspapers and scientific journals — were packed in barrels. Since John's mother had died in 1804, he claimed his portrait, which had been painted for her before he had departed for the New World. It, too, was crossing the Atlantic in its ornate carved wood and gilded frame. The most prized gift, and the one he hoped would dazzle Susan, was a solid sterling silver service set that included a tea pot, tray, sugar boat, cream pitcher and twenty-four sterling silver spoons, forks and knives, all engraved with a crest that he had devised — a crane, two elk heads, and the words *vive ut postea vivas* — "Live that you may truly live hereafter."

Jane, too, brought presents — which she carried in a basket hanging over her arm in the carriage to the seaport, across the moody Atlantic, and in the canoe all the way from Montreal to the Sault. Her precious gifts were cuttings from her aunt's gardens which would be planted before the front door of their home beside the Saint Marys River. The pinks were for Eliza — Wahbunnungoquay, or Morning Star Woman — while the bachelor buttons were for Lewis, the sweet william was for George, and a rose cutting was for Charlotte — Ogenebugoquay, or Woman of the Wild Rose. The hyacinth bulbs were for her mother, Neengay.

The journey home was energizing because John and Jane were returning to the land they loved, but it also was long. As they made their way westward through the lakes, the appearance of pine trees brought special joy to Jane's heart. Finally, in November, they made their way to the Saint Marys River. So intense were their feelings about returning home, and so accurately was their return anticipated, that Susan, acting on a premonition, dispatched a boat to meet them.

10

Invasion

It was an oppressively hot July afternoon in 1814 when Susan, tired after a morning of work, lay down to take an afternoon nap beside William and the infant Anna in the upstairs bedroom of their neat white house in the steadily growing village of Sault Sainte Marie.

Her first thoughts were about John, gone again this summer with a force of Canadian boatmen and Indians from the Sault, bound for Mackinac Island to help defend the garrison against American soldiers. He and his friend Charles Ermatinger, a trader for the North West Company from the Canadian side of the river, had actually taken the island from the Americans two summers before, soon after the War of 1812 had erupted. Susan's worries were for Jane, who was there on the island, as well. But she was not worried for herself. After all, George was there with her, and although he was just a teenager, he was mature for his age and was almost as much help to her as a grown man would have been. The small dark heads beside her were damp from the summer heat, but the owners slept soundly and, soon, the mother was drowsing too.

Suddenly Susan awoke, startled. Had she had a bad dream? No, something was going on outside. There had been the rumble of distant thunder all afternoon, but these sounds were different. Guns were being fired and people were shouting and screaming. It sounded as if the noises were coming from across the river, so she arose and hurried to the window that faced the river.

On the opposite bank, all was confusion. Several fires were burning, and black smoke obliterated a good part of the view. Several heavily-laden canoes were putting out from the other shore. Susan ran downstairs and out to the dock, where George was standing with the other children and the workers.

"What is it, George?"

"I don't know, Mother. It's some kind of attack. Some are in uniforms, it looks like. We need to leave! Into the woods!" he commanded, the fear in his voice obvious.

"Why should we flee? Who would harm us?" Susan was bewildered. By this time she could see Mananowe — the Ojibway wife of Charles Ermatinger — in the first canoe coming toward her from the opposite bank. She was clutching her baby tightly.

"Run!" Mananowe screamed from the boat. "American soldiers are looting and burning everything!" Tears were streaming down her face. Her hair was wild, her clothing disheveled.

Susan ran into the house and sent young Eliza and her helper Polly to get the sleeping children upstairs, while she gathered her precious silverware and John's candelabra into a tablecloth.

"George, get the records in the storehouse!" Susan cried out as she thrust a bundle at one of her helpers. Frantically, she looked around to see what else she should take with her. As the din seemed to be coming closer, she snatched John's portrait from the wall and shouted, "Everyone, into the woods!" With the picture frame bouncing against her stomach, she ran behind the straggling parade of friends and family, even cows and horses which the boys were switching and chasing.

Deep in the woods, she gathered her children and they crouched, lay or huddled around her, everyone panting and tired. Shouting and shooting could be heard for a long time in the direction from which they had come. No one spoke when they saw and smelled smoke, but a grieving Susan tried to imagine what had brought on such a sudden and savage attack by the soldiers — American soldiers! Suddenly, a black cloud scudded across the tree tops accompanied by a furious wind, and then a thundershower burst upon the fugitives. As the rain pelted them like stinging needles, Susan pulled the smallest children under her ample skirts. Within minutes, everybody was thoroughly soaked from the torential downpour. But it was a warm rain, and suddenly the children in the little circle began to laugh at how funny they all looked, and soon the thunder rolled off over the distant hills, leaving as quickly as it had come upon them.

After the storm, all was quiet in the direction of their homes, so George and his Ojibway cousins were delegated to scout and report. They soon returned with the news that the Americans were gone. Some buildings at the trading post had been set on fire, but the rain had reduced the fire to a smoldering state. The Johnston's house had been looted and vandalized, while some other houses had been burned.

When the bedraggled band struggled home, they returned to black and smoking ruins. The barn had been spared, so the boys were sent to round up the cows in the woods. Mananowe and her family settled down in the barn for the night with the Johnstons. Susan found some vegetables from her garden to serve for supper. After drinking some warm fresh milk, and after the day's excitement, everyone but Susan was soon asleep on the fragrant hay. Susan tried to think about what she must do first in the morning, but even she could not keep her eyes open, and she surrendered to exhaustion.

The next day, after surveying the damage to the Ermatinger house, which was equal to that suffered by the Johnstons, Susan called upon her Ojibway relatives living at the Sault to help her and her friend. The young men and boys searched through the ruins for anything of value and carted away the unwanted debris. The young women located clothing, vegetables, berries and whatever else they could find to feed and clothe the refugees.

One day, as Susan was walking through her vandalized home, her foot kicked a strange-shaped object — her father's warclub! Although it was blackened on one side, its tough, smooth wood had not been consumed by the flames. Susan sank to her knees in the sooty rubble and began feeling here and there, and she began to pick up first one and then another of her image stones, the strange little pebbles which grew in the red clay banks of the Chequamegon — those image stones which she had carried here to the Sault as a reminder of her happy childhood days on the sandy spit. She turned some of the blackened stones over in her hands, looking at a baby in a cradle, a carrot, and several perfect balls, and for the first time since the tragic and unexplained assault had occurred, tears began to stream down her cheeks.

When John returned a few days later, new timbers were already being cut to rebuild what had been lost in the attack. John was touched, yet greatly saddened when he realized that many of his possessions had been saved from the fire — but that Susan and the others had not rescued much of her beloved treasures, other than her silverware.

11
Keeper of the Peace

A warm day in June of 1820 found Susan and her small army of household helpers, both Indian and white, busy in the Johnston cabin. The war with Britain was over now, and had been for several years, but John Johnston had remained ever a loyal British subject even though he and his family lived south of the Saint Marys River in what was now an uncontested territory of the United States. John was away again, this time in Ireland where he was attempting to sell his ancestral property so he could rebuild his trading post. George — dear George, in Susan's mind — was in charge of his father's business where their outpost of twenty or thirty buildings represented the largest settlement within the region where a significant variety of both travelers' services and European and American trade goods could be obtained. The business provided social amenities to travelers, in addition to the everyday commerce in furs, kettles, guns, flour, fish, and other staples.

George had invited Lewis Cass, Governor of the Territory of Michigan, and his party to dinner at the Johnston home that evening. Susan had the girls polishing the silver, scrubbing the floors, and cleaning the log walls, in addition to preparing the food for the meal. Even though they knew how to make a variety of dishes, Susan was always careful to serve some local favorites, including Indian dishes, when visitors to the settlement dined with them. Jane was baking a fancy cake for dessert. Susan herself polished the rosewood piano, which had been transported from New Haven, Connecticut, since she would not allow anyone else to touch this delicate instrument which brought the very music of heaven to her here on earth. It had been a miracle that it had traveled safely from so far away, and she refused to trust providence a second time.

As Susan began to ready the wild rice with venison for dinner, she wondered about the men who would be dining with them tonight. They had told George that they were on a scientific mission. Indeed, their party contained a botanist, a mineralogist, a topographer, and a journalist. But what should she make of the twenty soldiers who accompanied them? The governor had said that he and his men were on their way to discover the source of the Mississippi River, but Susan doubted this. Why, she thought, would anyone care where a river originated? Surely there was another reason, something to do with the Indians in the area, and they were using the excuse of searching for the source of a river to conceal their real reason for being there. But why? She had not heard of an Indian uprising by way of her Ojibway friends. There had been only skirmishes between the Ojibway and the Sioux in settling their disputes over who controlled trapping grounds, or as a result of their drinking too much rum.

Suddenly, Susan heard the sound of women screaming, children crying, and dogs barking. She flew out of the door and saw wild confusion on the riverbanks. The Americans' camp on the low bank of the river was awash in soldiers who were scurrying about and jingling ramrods into their muskets. Women and children were hurrying into the canoes, which always lay about the river bank in summer, and were shoving off into the river — all the while wailing and crying. The dogs left behind on the shore were howling, and all Susan could think of was the day the Americans under the command of Major Holmes had attacked and looted their post six summers ago.

Susan's heart was beating as if it would burst. She immediately thought of George, of the help he provided the last time the Sault was invaded. She ran to his office and met him coming out in haste.

"What is it, George?" she screamed.

"We accompanied Governor Cass to a council with the chiefs. The Americans want a small piece of land for a garrison. At the conclusion, when the interpreter threw tobacco on the ground, instead of handing it around, Sessaba kicked it and said not to accept tobacco thrown on the ground like bones are thrown to dogs. Sessaba has hoisted the British flag above his village! Cass has gone to the village, and his soldiers are readying their guns!"

"For God's sake, George, get Shinguacouse and Shingaba Wossin. Get the others, too! That foolish young Sessaba will bring his people to ruin. Get them here at once!"

A messenger was immediately dispatched, and in less than an hour the chiefs and elders of the Ojibway at the Sault were assembled in George's office.

The young man, fully aware that half of his blood was the same as theirs, while the rest of it was the same as that of the soldiers, stood before them and began to speak solemnly.

"My friends and relatives, I am young and possess very little wisdom to give you advice at the present time. It is from you that I should receive it, but on this occasion allow me to give you a few words of warning, and I do not plan to speak for long. You are all aware that hostilities between Great Britain and the United States have ceased. Peace now exists, and the two nations are living on friendly terms. One of your young men misbehaved and has given a gross insult to the Governor of Michigan, a representative of the President of the United States, by hoisting a British flag on his acknowledged territory. You cannot expect that the British government will sustain Sessaba in such an act. I understand that he has gone to arm himself and raise warriors. Be wise. Be quick and put a stop to his wild scheme and suppress the uprising of your young men. The firing of one gun will bring ruin to your tribe and to the Ojibway nation such that a dog will not be left to howl in your villages."

At this moment, Susan entered and, with all the authority of Waubojeeg's daughter and John Johnston's wife, said, "My brothers, the Americans came in peace. They have gained this very land we used to call our own by reason of a war with Britain. It is their land now. Quickly, quickly, stop the ill-advised actions of Sessaba at once, before blood is shed. It will then be too late!"

Shingaba Wossin stood and agreed with Susan and George, and suggested that Shinguacouse — Little Pine, the tribal orator and a warrior who had fought with the British during the war — would be the best person to try to calm Sessaba. The elders agreed and selected some other braves to accompany him to find Sessaba and to order him, on behalf of the tribe, to stop his aggression. The delegation left and moved quickly along the portage road, where they soon met the temperamental Sessaba. He had been wearing a British uniform earlier in the day, but now he was in war paint and feathers and was leading a party of similarly-clad young warriors. Shinguacouse told them that he had been authorized by the chiefs and elders to put a stop to Sessaba's proceedings. "You were one of our leaders when the Americans felled my brother in battle. How dare you stop my revenge!" Sessaba shouted as he hurled his war club at Shinguacouse. The weapon grazed Shinguacouse's left shoulder, but instead of enraging him, as it was meant to do, it only made him all the more eloquent in presenting his arguments. For now, he saw clearly that all Ojibways would suffer because of one man's pain and his need to avenge his brother's death. Shinguacouse talked quietly and argued persuasively, and after a long time, Sessaba and his group slowly dispersed and returned to a quiet village.

The chiefs were notified of the encounter, as were George and Susan immediately thereafter. "Now, George, they must present an apology to Governor Cass or this thing will not end satisfactorily," Susan said. That afternoon the chiefs and the governor met in George's office, the neutral ground. They apologized for the emotional behavior of Sessaba, and the governor accepted it. Once calm had been restored, the business originally intended for the morning got underway. By the end of the day, the treaty of June 16, 1820, was consummated between both parties. The Sault Ojibway had ceded four square miles to the United States government for a garrison, but they had reserved the right to hunt and fish at the rapids in perpetuity. At the conclusion of the treaty, George sent for two bottles of old Madeira and some tobacco, and those present who drank pledged themselves to keep the treaty. The treaty was sealed properly, in Ojibway fashion, by passing the peace pipe around to so that all in attendance could smoke and thereby confirm their acceptance of the agreement.

That evening, the governor, accompanied by Lieutenant Pierce, Mr. Douglass, and Mr. Henry Rowe Schoolcraft, arrived at the Johnston home for dinner. Even though the evening was warm, Susan wore her best blue skirt over many petticoats and a long-sleeved darker coat with lace at the neck. Her hair was pulled back straight and knotted at the nape of her neck. George and Susan met the guests at the door and introduced them to Jane, her hair lying smooth across her forehead with tight curls dancing around her neck, and dressed in a dotted mull gown. Although Susan understood English and laughed her low, happy laugh as the visitors talked and joked, she spoke only Ojibway that evening and George and Susan translated for the gentlemen. The officers were impressed with her dignity and grace of speech.

There was a sense of relaxation and good feeling among the guests now that the day's danger had passed, in part because, while they were dining and drinking French wine from Montreal, they knew the soldiers were keeping a close watch for any threatening activity in the Ojibway village. All remained calm outside, however, and the gathering within the Johnston home was enjoyable for the visitors who were surprised by the hospitality and level of refinement they were experiencing on this remote frontier of American settlement. Here candles rested in sterling silver candlesticks, and they used real silverware when eating their fruit compote. The dishes upon which their roasted venison was served were Blue Willow, and the wine was served in Waterford crystal. After dinner, Jane played the piano accompanied by George on the flute.

As he readied himself for bed that night, one of the Americans, Henry Rowe Schoolcraft, mused on what a curious day it had been — starting with the unexpected danger and excitement of the morning and

Henry Rowe Schoolcraft later in life. (Courtesy H. R. Schoolcraft Papers, Bentley Historical Collection, University of Michigan, Ann Arbor, Michigan.)

concluding with the calm and exquisite pleasure of dining with the Johnstons in the evening. This was indeed a place of extreme contrasts, and he was enjoying himself immensely.

Schoolcraft had been fascinated by his introduction to the land about the Sault and its inhabitants, just as he was relishing the arduous trip he was on in the company of Governor Cass. Schoolcraft had established a reputation as a geologist from his experience in his family's glass factory in New York. His description of his exploration of the lead mines in Missouri had been published in 1819, and this had led to his appointment as geologist with the expedition of Governor Cass to seek the source of the Mississippi River. By the time that the party had reached Sault Sainte Marie, it had already navigated sections of the coasts of lakes Huron and Michigan. After leaving the Sault, the group followed the south shore of Lake Superior to its westernmost end at Fond du Lac, then followed voyageur routes up the Saint Louis River to the Wisconsin River. Returning to Lake Michigan at Green Bay, Cass and his fellows retraced their route on Lake Huron to Detroit.

Schoolcraft had no opportunity to see the Johnston's again that year, but he had taken special notice of Jane and his mind frequently turned to thoughts of her. He particularly valued an image of her sitting at the little rosewood piano, shoulders bare and curls bobbing in the candlelight while she played.

Upon completion of the exploration, Schoolcraft returned to New York in the fall and worked on his

Narrative Journal, which was published in 1821. Both the success of Schoolcraft's *Narrative Journal* and Governor Cass's high regard for the young man figured in Schoolcraft's appointment as the new Indian agent for the United States government at Sault Sainte Marie in the summer of 1822.

On July 16, he was invited to have dinner with the Johnstons, and a month later he moved into a room in their home — into Lewis Saurin's room. Now he had frequent opportunities to see Jane at the piano! However, it was not until December 29th of that year that Henry was invited to attend the family's evening worship service.

Susan and John had been married according to Ojibway custom in 1792, but it was not until 1821 that they celebrated a Christian marriage. That service had been performed by James Winniett, and at that time Ozhaguscodaywayquay had officially taken the name of Susan. She was now his wife and, according to European and American customs, should John die, she and their children were legally entitled to inherit his estate. John had always maintained a deep sense of religious faith here so far from the formal Christian clergy and church properties. He read the Bible every morning and evening, even when on long canoe trips.

And so it happened this cold winter evening when Charlotte placed a cushion for John to kneel upon after he read from the Bible, and as the Irish Indian went down on his knees, the whole family followed his example. For many long, silent moments, all bowed their heads and said personal prayers, and then John thanked the Lord for the many blessings he had bestowed on their family — the full storehouse for the winter, the good hunting, the general good health of the family, the gift of intellect, and even the presence of good friends. Schoolcraft felt a special warmth about all of this. The circle of light from the fireplace and lamp, the dark shiny heads bowed, and the graceful civility of the entire family all combined to make such an impression on Henry that he yearned to become a part of this group in a more permanent fashion than merely an honored boarder. And so it came to be, for in October, 1823, the Reverend R. M. Laird united in marriage Miss Jane Johnston — Obahbahm-Wawa-Geshagoquay, The Sound the Stars Make Rushing Through the Sky — to Henry Rowe Schoolcraft.

A year later, William Henry Schoolcraft was born, and Henry was indeed welded firmly to this remarkable family. Sadly, Sweet William died of croup two and a half years later, but Jane Susan Anne was born in 1827 and John Johnston Schoolcraft in 1829.

Henry Rowe Schoolcraft had married into a family famous for their storytelling ability. Less than a month after his establishment at the Sault, he had noticed the mythological character of the Ojibway oral tales and that they often taught some truth or maxim. He began eagerly to gather the fanciful stories with the help of his mother-in-law, his wife Jane, and her brother George. Susan, especially, facilitated Henry's access to the information for which he so yearned. Schoolcraft himself wrote:

> Mrs. Johnston is a woman of excellent judg-
> ment and good sense; she is referred to on abstruse
> points of the Indian ceremonies and usages, so that
> I have in fact stumbled, as it were, on the only fam-
> ily in North West America who could, in Indian lore,
> have acted as my "guide, philosopher and friend"
> (Osborn and Osborn, 404).

But it would take seventeen years before Schoolcraft's collection of Ojibway tales, *Algic Researches,* was published, and even more time would pass before other writings about the Ojibway and other Indians made their way into print. During the time Schoolcraft was stationed at the Sault, he served not only as Indian agent but also was elected to two terms on the Legislative Council of Michigan Territory, was appointed to the first Board of Regents of the University of Michigan, and for a time was Superintendent of Indian Affairs at Detroit.

Schoolcraft's writings were popular in the East, and they eventually came to the attention of Henry Wadsworth Longfellow who pored over the oral tales of the Ojibway and other Indians which had been collected by Schoolcraft. It was Schoolcraft's publications, in great part, which inspired and provided the factual material for Longfellow's influential poem *The Song of Hiawatha*, published in 1855.

Ozhaguscodaywayquay introduced Henry Rowe Schoolcraft to the great depth and breadth of Ojibway culture, and Longfellow drew extensively from Schoolcraft's information in writing *The Song of Hiawatha*. The first British edition of *Hiawatha* included this image of Hiawatha leaving Nokomis to search for his father. (Courtesy National Park Service, Longfellow National Historic Site, Cambridge, Massachusetts.)

The poet Henry Wadsworth Longfellow as he appeared in 1855, the year that *The Song of Hiawatha* was first published. (Courtesy National Park Service, Longfellow National Historic Site, Cambridge, Massachusetts.)

12
Path of Souls

J ust as the coming of the Europeans to Ojibway lands in the late 18th century brought upheaval to the ancient ways of Indian life, so too the arrival of the 19th century brought unrest and change to the lives of the pale-skinned newcomers. Three issues in particular seemed to converge upon the upper Great Lakes frontier during the second decade of the 19th century — issues that affected most residents of the region as they struggled to accommodate the new political and economic order. The fur-bearing animals had been over-harvested for years, and as a result this resource was becoming scarce and competition for the diminishing supply was increasing. Simultaneously, the beaver hats for which so many of the beaver pelts had been used were going out of style in Europe, so demand for one of the most important products of the upper Great Lakes region was diminishing. And following the treaties that ended the wars between Great Britain and the American colonists and the War of 1812, both governments were intent on establishing definite boundaries and extending sovereignty to these boundaries, even in the wilderness.

It was a reflection of the social turmoil of the times that John Johnston, a British subject living in an American frontier town, had taken part in a British attack on the American garrison at Mackinac Island during the War of 1812 while he was serving as Justice of the Peace for areas under control of the United States government — and that an American army had destroyed John Johnston's property, on American soil, in 1814. Also, independent fur traders could no longer compete with the larger trading companies, so for a while Johnston was affiliated with the large American Fur Company of John Jacob Astor and Ramsay Crooks. After the United States Congress passed a law stipulating that only American citizens could trade on American soil, however, Johnston was excluded from practicing what had been his life's work.

In 1816, Johnston had tried to obtain compensation for the losses he had suffered that July day in 1814 when Major Holmes attacked his home and buildings at the Sault, but the Lieutenant Governor of Canada informed him that his request was too late. In 1819, Johnston had presented his claim to Lord Commissioner of His Majesty's Treasury in London, but nothing came of it since his post was south of the international border now fixed by treaty. And the American government refused to pay Johnston for the damages because he was a British citizen. In an effort to reestablish himself, Johnston had sold his ancestral

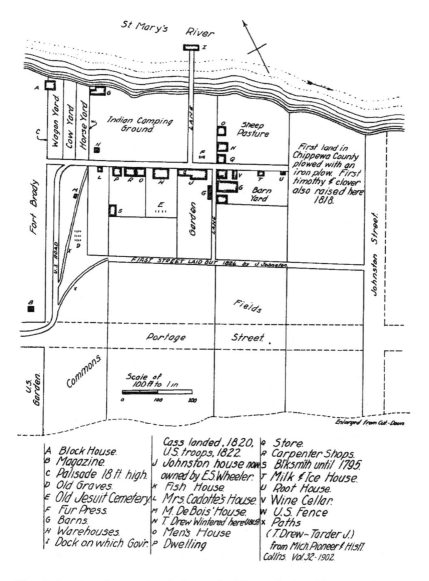

The Johnston homestead about 1825, as derived from a sketch of the property by John McDougall Johnston, the youngest of Susan and John's children. (Courtesy Judge Joseph H. Steere Room, Bayliss Public Library, Sault Sainte Marie, Michigan.)

A Description of Susan Johnston in 1827

Mrs. Johnson [sic] is a genuine Chippeway, without the smallest admixture of white blood. She is tall and large, but uncommonly active and cheerful. She dresses nearly in the costume of her nation — blue petticoat, of cloth, a short-gown of calico, with leggins worked with beads, and moccasins. Her hair is black. She plaits and fastens it up behind with a comb. Her eyes are black and expressive, and pretty well marked . . . . As it is, she is a prodigy. As a wife, she is devoted to her husband; — as a mother, tender and affectionate; — as a friend, faithful. She manages her domestic concerns in a way that might afford lessons to the better instructed. They are rarely exceeded any where, — whilst she vies with her generous husband in his hospitality to strangers. She understands, but will not speak English. As to influence, there is no chief in the Chippeway nation who exercises it, when it is necessary for her to do so, with equal success. This has often been tested, but especially at the treaty of cession at this place, in 1820. . . .

I have heard Governor Cass say that he felt himself then, and does yet, under the greatest obligation to Mrs. J. for her co-operation at that critical moment; and that the United States are debtor to her, not only on account of that act, but on many others. — She has never been known in a single instance, to council her people but in accordance with her conceptions of what was best for them, and never in opposition to the views of the government. Her Indian name is Oshauguscodaywayqua.

(from McKenney, 1827)

estate in Ireland in 1820, but the proceeds from this sale only enabled him to engage in a small trade with the locals; the major commerce in the area was now monopolized by the American Fur Company.

As his debts increased, this man of manners who had always placed intellect above emotions, was being reduced to a complaining old man — a role he hated yet felt compelled to assume in order to provide adequately for his still growing family. Thus, John Johnston had traveled to New York during the summer of 1828 to try one last time to obtain compensation for the wanton destruction of his twenty year's of labor, but this effort, too, proved futile.

And so it was a disappointed and disgruntled man who traveled from New York City up the Hudson River, across New York State via the Erie Canal, then on across Lake Erie and Lake Huron to the Saint Marys River. On the last three days of the trip, John could hold no food in his stomach, and a doctor aboard the ship spent all of his time with the Irishman. At the Sault, John was carried from the boat directly to his home. Susan at once tried every remedy she knew of, those of the Indian and White Man, but despite her best efforts, John only grew weaker. Susan sent word by sailboat to George, who was at LaPointe, that his father was in very poor health.

Charlotte, Eliza, Anna Maria, John McDougall, and William hovered around their father and mother, but John was so weak by now that he could only tell Susan that his trip had been in vain. He then lapsed into a coma and never regained consciousness. At 8 P.M. on

September 22nd, with Susan beside him holding his hand, John Johnston, Irish Indian, died.

Susan had said all of her goodbyes, and had re-lived their good and bad times together as she sat beside him, day and night, for the three days before his death. Only she would know that the last official rebuff of their efforts to obtain compensation for Major Holmes's actions had played a role in hastening John's final moments. The doctor would say his death was caused by "typhoid," while the family declared the causes to be "dysentery and old age," but Susan knew in her heart that it was his final admission of defeat that broke his spirit. All that he had worked for had been destroyed in a single senseless and irresponsible act, and he believed that his life had been lived for nothing.

Because husbands and wives did not say such things to each other, she had never expressed her feelings to John. But, as she had sat beside the gray and gasping man, her husband and lover, she had felt that their whole life together had been beautiful and meaningful, indeed, even mystic — their's the way two such different people should have come together and lived as one. What matter the winepress, the furpress, the windmill and the buildings? There were eight fine children to show for their thirty-six years together, and now there were even grandchildren, too — George's Louisa, John and William, and Jane's baby, Jane Susan. Yes, she and John worked hard, but their life together had been good and it had made the children healthy. With John's death, the younger boys would not get the education in Montreal or Ireland that the others had, but still the older ones who were now well situated could help the younger ones get good jobs. After all, was not Jane's husband Henry in the Michigan Territorial Legislature?

After a sigh, Susan arose to call her cousin to help her prepare the body for the visitation of friends and relatives who would be coming. The continuous line of faces, both red and white, that filled her house, the meals for relatives, and the religious service for John were all a blur to Susan, Woman of the Green Glade. Her children were solicitous, but she did not cry; she held her head up, befitting the wife of a well-to-do and respected businessman. As the wooden coffin was lowered into its place beside "Sweet William" Schoolcraft's grave in the cemetery and, as the shovelfuls of dirt were thrown over it, the last thing she saw was the silver teaspoon John had so proudly brought her from Ireland so many years ago, beaten flat now, and affixed to the coffin, engraved:

John Johnston ESQ.
born Ireland Aug. 25, 1762
died Sept. 22, 1828
aged 66 years 27 days

13
Laying Down the Burden

Querulous crows cawing from a tree branch outside her bedroom window awakened Susan one morning in March, 1837. She hurried to dress and have her breakfast, for today she was going to collect maple syrup.

Her pack, with cedar and basswood spiles, hatchet and light containers, had been readied the night before. Now, she put on her warm coat, deerskin leggings and moccasins, tied on her snowshoes, and with the pack on her back, she hiked to her island — Sugar Island, located in the Saint Marys River a short distance downstream from her cabin. Sugar Island had been granted to her by the United States government as an expression of gratitude for her assistance to Governor Cass in concluding the treaty with the Ojibway in 1822. She deemed this island the most valuable of all lands because it was covered with maple trees, the source of the valuable maple sugar. Eliza would come later in the day with various Ojibway relatives and servants; their job would be to carry the heavy iron kettles and barrels across the snow-covered river on toboggans pulled by dogs. But Susan couldn't wait to begin the process — someone had to open the holes in the trees and insert the spiles to get the sap flowing, so she set off alone to get this part of the work done.

The day was foggy, and the whole earth seemed to be enveloped in silver. Hoarfrost covered every branch and tree, and they, too, had a dully silver gleam. The sun was trying to break through the misty envelope but only succeeded in turning the whole world into a kind of luminous golden mist. The only other color in this monochromatic landscape was the bright red branches of the willow and ninebark trees and shrubs. The warm sun of the past few days had baked a crust on the snow, and Susan thought, as she trudged along, "Our ancestors were right to call this the Month of Broken Snowshoes!"

All of a sudden she heard the distinctive sound of the woodpecker working at the bark of a tree trunk. "That means warm weather," she thought. "We must hurry; the sap will only keep a day or two if this continues, then it will sour."

Crows called all around her and she shouted back to them, "Caw! Caw! You are rightly calling us to the trees; if this warm weather continues the maples will keep the juice for their own buds. It will become yellow and bitter, and will be of no use to us!"

As she traveled farther, she thought of her daugh-

Neengay in the Garden by Ralph A. Wolfe is located in Sault Sainte Marie, Michigan. This statue, dedicated in 1988, portrays Neengay picking berries from her garden, a favorite activity and a scene fondly remembered by her children and grandchildren. The owl and fisher commemorate her father, Waubojeeg, White Fisher, and remind of her status as the daughter of a great Ojibway leader. (Photograph by Jack Soetebier.)

ter Jane. This beloved child now lived on Mackinac Island where her husband was the Indian agent for the United States government. Jane's children, Jane Susan and John Johnston, were grandchildren to be proud of. And, George, dear George, was with her now that his wife had died. His sons were now more men than boys, almost as old as their father had been when the soldiers had burned their trading post. Susan still became sad when she thought about that event, even after all the years that had passed, but she was not bitter as John had been. Yet, she was convinced that the attack by Major Holmes had broken him. Yes, the devastation of his life's work and the unresponsiveness of the American government, a government he had supported and respected, had been the cause of his death. She remembered now how distraught the family had been at his funeral. The family had sold his trading post stores and buildings to satisfy his debts, and at the end, she had only her home by the riverside and the Irish china and silverware left. How would she live? Her family worried.

"Well, I will raise vegetables in the garden as I have always done," she had told them. "The cows will still give milk, and the berries will grow in summer. Perhaps one of my sons will bring me a little venison now and then. And I will go with my people in the spring and fall to the creeks and bays along the lake to take the whitefish." It seemed so simple to her.

"But taxes, Neengay," her sons protested. "You will need to pay taxes on your land, or the State of Michigan will take it away from you!" This concept of

114

taxes was new to her; in earlier times, the land had just been there.

"Well, then, I shall make maple syrup and maple sugar to sell!" she had retorted. And so she had, every year since John had died. The white people settling at the Sault liked the maple syrup, but they did not have title to the land with the maple trees. She, however, did — for the Treaty of Fond du Lac in 1826 had given her part of the highlands of Sugar Island.

And so, here she was again, in her private forest. She began driving the spiles into the holes left from last years' sugaring, and immediately the dripping sound of the running sap falling into her small buckets could be heard. She gathered branches and began making a pile of them by her fire. She was just beginning to stomp down the snow in the area of the cook shack, whose skeleton of saplings had been left from last year, when she heard shouting and barking in the distance. "Oh, it's going to be the best crop ever!" she shouted to Eliza, as soon as she caught sight of her sturdy daughter through the trees. "Hurry, the sap is running!"

Eliza and the others arrived and set about preparing the kettles. No sooner was the largest kettle installed over the fire than Susan was already emptying the small containers of sap into it. The adults were busy reconstructing the cook shack and unpacking the equipment while the children, laughing and squealing, chased the dogs around and around the snowy area designated for the sleeping lodge. Next, the boys were sent on errands to find evergreen branches for mattresses. By supper time, everybody was rewarded for their help with the first bit of maple sugar to suck on. Susan had been working the boiled syrup with a wooden paddle in a large birchbark mokuk. "The first is always the best!" she assured them.

By dark, all were exhausted and bedded down on the fragrant branches — except Susan. She was checking to see that the fire had enough wood and that all of the containers had been emptied. Finally, she went around to the hot bubbling kettles with a long stick that had a bit of bear fat on the end. By thrusting the fat into the steam, she was performing an ancient ritual which stopped the syrup from boiling over the sides of the kettle.

As Eliza settled down in her blanket and positioned herself for sleep, she thought, "That Neengay! She thinks every batch of syrup will be the best ever! Just as she thinks each new grandchild will be the best ever! There she is yet, after hiking all the way here today and working all day, still trying to see that no smoke curls into the syrup and that no ice forms in the shallow buckets. At her age! She should leave that to younger workers. But, of course, she's afraid that none will do it as well as she!"

It was a good year for maple sugar — maybe the best ever. Susan and her family manufactured 3,500 pounds of it that spring, more than enough to pay the land taxes.

~

As the years of her waning life passed, Susan often went to the cemetery; more of her family and friends were there now — perhaps, it sometimes seemed, more than were alive. At every visit, she remembered not only those whose headstones were evident, but those whom she had loved dearly who had been buried elsewhere. Jane, her beloved Jane, her first daughter, more like a sister to her than child, lay in Ancaster, Ontario. And Lewis, her first son, her delight — she thought about that day in February when he and a party of fellow naval officers had come by snowshoe forty-five miles across the ice from Fort Drummond just to surprise them with a visit — so soon after he had been wounded the summer before. His grave in Amherstburg, Ontario, was another which she would never see in this life. John's grave, however, was the object of most of her attention. She cleared away the weeds and planted cuttings from the plants that grew beside the front door of her home. But Shingaba Wossin's grave also knew her presence; the little wooden grave house was now weathered and gray, but within it rested the remnants of her image stones from the land of her childhood. Sweet William slept beside John, and Monsieur and Madame Cadotte, who had treated her like a member of their own family when she and John had first come from the Island of the Golden Breasted Woodpecker, were also at rest here. Her thoughts turned often these days to that enchanted spot at LaPointe where her life with John began, and it was there that her own mother was buried along with Waubojeeg and the grandmother.

The fall winds of 1843 caused the elderly, heavyset Woman of the Green Glade to pull her shawl tighter about her shoulders as she walked slowly home. A year ago, her youngest child, John McDougall, had married and she was coming to feel that her job in life was done. She looked around her at the dry lifeless leaves on the ground and at the trees, now almost bare-branched, and she felt the way she had at her father's funeral — as if she were seeing something for the last time. Then, suddenly, the sun emerged from behind the clouds and shone on the wide, still river below her and the golden maple trees covering the opposite bank and the hills beyond it. The sudden brilliance turned the river to a sheet of shimmering silver, the hills to dazzling gold. Ozhaguscodaywayquay smiled at this largesse of the Kitchi Manitou. These were her riches, and no one could take them away from her — this river of silver, these hills of gold.

Epilogue

28 November, 1843

Dear George,

    <u>Your mother is dead</u>! Her spirit returned to the power that caused its being this morning at about 11 o'clock. To moralize upon the event of <u>Death</u> will be left more to your imagination than to my pen. It will be sufficient for me to say that <u>Your Mother is Dead</u> and another Mother you can never have. A Mother, unlike a wife, husband, a brother or a sister can never be replaced.

    The night before last she was attacked with an oppression of the stomach, which threatened suffocation, for which the doctor bled and gave medicine. During the following day she was easier, but on the next night, near day, she sent for Maria, and the doctor was called, who again bled her and applied the cupping glass and administered other remedies. At breakfast she said she felt better and the next I heard was of her death. She died in Maria's arms, suddenly, from suffocation while the doctor was at her side. The doctor informed me that the upper orifice of the windpipe became closed. He tried

119

to inflate the lungs with a pipe stem, but was unable, and before a proper instrument could be procured from the Fort, she expired.

A few moments before her death she retired and spent some time in prayer and signified her perfect preparation for Death. The only absent one she expressed a wish to see <u>was yourself</u>. She said she would like to have talked with you before she left the World.

Her only pain in going was, she said, that Ev and Howard would come, as they are in the house every morning to see Grandma, and Grandma would be gone.

Her funeral will take place on the 30th in the morning and need I assure you that all respect will be paid in carrying her to the final resting place at the side of your much lamented Father.

Yours truly
J. L. Schoolcraft

And so James L. Schoolcraft, brother of Henry Rowe Schoolcraft and husband of Anna Maria Johnston, described the passing of his mother-in-law, Ozhaguscodaywayquay, Woman of the Green Glade, to the path of the souls on November 28, 1843. The death of Ozhaguscodaywayquay ended the life of a noteworthy woman.

∽

Ozhaguscodaywayquay and John Johnston are both buried in Riverside Cemetery, Sault Sainte Marie, Michigan. Although all of the Johnston's first house has been lost, that portion of their second home which was added for the newly wedded Jane and Henry Schoolcraft in 1823 survives and incorporates the west wall of the original second house and its hewn sill timbers. The surviving structure is now a National Historic Site. Following completion of renovations and repairs underway during the summer of 1999, this building will be open to the public and several of the Johnston's personal items will be on display.

The Charles Oakes Ermatinger home on the Canadian side of the river has been completely and beautifully restored and is open to the public.

The River of History Museum in Sault Sainte Marie, Michigan, tells the story of the Johnston family and the history of the Sault region.

Susan used her sugarbush on Sugar Island until her death. The United States census of 1930 shows that 918 people lived on the island at that time, and half of them were Ojibway. Sugar Island is still a popular place to live today.

Madeline Island in the Apostle Islands is today a popular summer destination for visitors and residents. The Indian graveyard near the Madeline Island Marina may be visited, and the history of the region is interpreted at the Madeline Island Historical Museum.

The falls of Saint Croix are no longer; a hydroelectric dam was built downstream from this site earlier this century. However, a short distance below the dam the rocky sides of the river must still look as they did two hundred years ago when Waubojeeg successfully led his warriors against the Sioux.

The Johnston House in Sault Sainte Marie. The original Johnston house was built in 1794 and damaged or destroyed in 1814. A second house was built on the same site in 1815 using the French-Canadian style of chamfered logs, and an addition was made in 1823 in which Jane and her husband, Henry Rowe Schoolcraft, lived until 1827. The surviving portion of the house is the 1823 addition; its west wall is the chamfered east wall of the 1815 house. (Photograph by Jack Soetebier.)

Glossary

ANISHINABE: the original or spontaneous people

BOW-E-TING: the Sault Sainte Marie area, Michigan and Canada

KINICKINICK: Indian tobacco; tree bark

KITCHI GAMI: Lake Superior

KITCHI MANITOU: Great Spirit; God

INAENDAUGWUT: it is permitted; fate

MANITOU: spirit; inspiration

MANOMIN: wild rice

MATCHI MANITOU: evil spirit; devil

MIDE MEGIS: sacred seashell

MEGIS: white seashell

MIDEWEGUN: lodge of the Medicine Society

MIDEWEWIN: Grand Medicine Society; religion

MOKUK: birch bark container

NAWADJIWON: in the middle of the stream; undecided

PINDGIGOSSAN: medicine bag; usually an otter skin

TIKINAGAN: cradleboard for infant

WATTAP: twine made of pine roots

WIGUB: twine made from basswood

WHITE MAN'S MILK: rum; other spirits

Bibliography

Arbic, Bernard J. 1992. *Sugar Island Sampler: A Slice of Upper Peninsula Heritage*. Allegan Forest, MI: Priscilla Press.

Baraga, Frederic. 1992 [1878]. *A Dictionary of the Ojibway Language*. Saint Paul, MN: Minnesota Historical Society Press.

Densmore, Frances. 1979 [1929]. *Chippewa Customs*. Saint Paul, MN: Minnesota Historical Society Press.

Dewdney, Selwyn. 1975. *The Sacred Scrolls of the Southern Ojibway*. Toronto, ONT: University of Toronto Press for The Glenbow-Alberta Institute, Calgary, Alberta.

Drake, Samuel G. 1848. *Biography and History of the Indians of North America from Its First Discovery*. Tenth edition. Boston, MA: Benjamin B. Mussey, & Co.

Hambleton, Elizabeth, and Elizabeth Warren Stoutamire. 1992. *The John Johnston Family of*

Sault Ste. Marie. N.p.: The Johnston Family Assn.

Johnston, Basil. 1976. *Ojibway Heritage.* Toronto, ONT: McCleland and Stewart LTD.

Johnston, George. 1908. "Reminiscences." *Historical Collections, Pioneer Society of the State of Michigan,* volume XII, pp. 608–611.

Kohl, Johann Georg. 1985 [1860]. *Kitchi-Gami: Life Among the Lake Superior Ojibway.* Saint Paul, MN: Minnesota Historical Society Press.

Longfellow, Henry Wadsworth. 1855. *The Song of Hiawatha.* Boston, MA: Ticknor and Fields.

MacDonald, Graham A. 1981. "Commerce, Civility and Old Sault Ste. Marie." *The Beaver: Magazine of the North,* volume 312 (3: Winter): pp. 52–59.

McKenney, Thomas L. 1827. *Sketches of a Tour to the Lakes, of the Character and Customs of the Chippeway Indians, and of Incidents Connected with the Treaty of Fond du Lac.* Baltimore, MD: F. Lucas, Jr.

Nute, Grace Lee. 1944. *Lake Superior.* Indianapolis, IN: Bobbs-Merrill Company.

Osborn, Chase S., and Stellanova Osborn. 1942. *Schoolcraft, Longfellow, Hiawatha.* Lancaster, PA: Jaques Cattell Press.

Ross, Hamilton Nelson. 1960. *La Pointe, Village Outpost.* Saint Paul, MN: North Central Publishing Company.

Schoolcraft, Henry Rowe. 1821. *Narrative Journal of Travels Through the Northwestern Regions of the United*

States; Extending From Detroit Through the Great Chain of American Lakes, to the Sources of the Mississippi River. Albany, NY: E. & E. Hosford.

——. 1839. *Algic Researches: Comprising Inquiries Respecting the Mental Characteristics of the North American Indians : First Series : Indian Tales and Legends.* New York, NY: Harper.

——. 1851. *Personal Memoirs of a Residence of Thirty Years with the Indian Tribes on the American Frontiers; with Brief Notices of Passing Events, Facts, and Opinions, A.D. 1812 to A.D. 1842.* Philadelphia, PA: Lippincott, Grambo & Company.

——. 1851–1857. *Historical and Statistical Information Respecting the History, Condition, and Prospects of the Indian Tribes of the United States.* Philadelphia, PA: Lippincott, Grambo.

——. 1853. *Western Scenes and Reminiscences: together with Thrilling Legends and Traditions of the Red Men of the Forest.* Buffalo, NY: Derby, Orton & Mulligan.

——. 1962 [1826–1827]. *The Literary Voyager; or, Muzzeniegun.* Philip P. Mason, editor. East Lansing, MI: Michigan State University Press.

——. 1982. *The Historic Johnston Family of Sault Ste. Marie, Michigan.* Iron Mountain, MI: Mid-Peninsula Library Cooperative.

Warren, William W. 1984. *History of the Ojibway People. Collections of the Minnesota Historical Society*, volume 5. Saint Paul, MN: Minnesota Historical Society Press.

Index